The 21st
CENTURY
MAN

The 21st CENTURY MAN

Learning How to Succeed in Changing Times

BISHOP L. W. FRANCISCO III

THE 21st CENTURY MAN: LEARNING HOW TO SUCCEED IN
CHANGING TIMES

Cover Design by Atinad Designs

© Copyright 2009

SAINT PAUL PRESS, DALLAS, TEXAS
First Printing, 2009

Unless otherwise indicated, all verses are taken from the King James
Version (KJV) of the Bible.

Scripture taken from The Message. Copyright© 1993, 1994, 1995,
1996, 2000, 2001, 2002. Used by permission of NavPress Publishing
Group.

Scripture quotations taken from the Amplified® Bible, Copyright ©
1954, 1958, 1962, 1964, 1965, 1987 by The Lockman Foundation.
Used by permission.

The name SAINT PAUL PRESS and its logo are registered as a
trademark in the U.S. patent office.

ISBN-13: 978-0-9825303-2-0

Printed in the U.S.A.

CONTENTS

ACKNOWLEDGEMENTS

I WOULD LIKE TO FIRST ACKNOWLEDGE MY Lord and Savior Who has allowed me to experience life in a way I never dreamed imaginable. God has blessed me beyond measure, and I have the privilege of sharing insights in this book that I trust will bless the life of every reader.

I want to thank my wife, Natalie, of 26 years for allowing me the opportunity to be who I am as God has molded and shaped me. May God bless you as you enter a new season of destiny. ("You go, Woman of Wisdom, Worth and Worship!") To our daughters, Nicole, Lesley and Lauren: each of you have allowed me to be a father and a mentor and now I learn from you. To my mother, Naomi Francisco, and father, the late Bishop L. W. Francisco II who gave me a solid understanding of manhood, for which I am grateful. To my brother, Myron, thanks for all you do that allows me to focus on preaching the Gospel.

To Sister Linder Hunn, you invested your time and talents in this project, and for that I thank you. To my administrative assistant, Cyndi and office manager, Xiomara, thank you for working in concert with Linder. To all of my staff and church family, each of you have contributed to my life in special ways that help to make what I do possible. I thank each of you for your support and belief in the vision.

To all my covenant Pastors: the Prides, the Ranchods and

the Carrolls, may God continue to bless and increase the anointing and call on your lives and ministries. I am grateful for the experiences that we have shared as we expand God's Kingdom.

Finally, I want to acknowledge my late brother, Steven Francisco. To God be the glory. (I miss you, man.)

PRAISE FOR
THE 21ST CENTURY MAN

Wow! I simply loved this book. I couldn't put it down once I started it. Seldom does a book say it better or more powerfully than *The 21st Century Man*. This book is a must read for those who want to navigate the slippery slope of succeeding in business and life in tough times. My heartfelt thanks goes out to Bishop L. W. Francisco III for giving us this important gem and then challenging us to live in a good and righteous way. Thank you, Bishop Francisco, for this gift.

—George Fraser
CEO, FraserNet, Inc.
Author, *Click: 10 Truths For Building Extraordinary Relationships*

The enemy of our soul wants to stop every man from knowing his rightful place in God. What may even be worse is to know God's plan for your life, but you can't fulfill it because you feel confused, overwhelmed or powerless.

With godly wisdom, Bishop Francisco is gifted at revealing powerful and life changing truths that are born out of experience in the Word of God. Inspiring, enlightening, and empowering truths that give you the tools you need to change those things that may be holding you back.

The 21st Century Man will give you a clear personal blueprint to help you get your breakthrough and get you where you need to go in your life. Even as I read the book, I had many of those "aha" moments! One of those was "the secret of the cave." Wow! Read it. You'll see.

If you want to get on track and begin to get your power back, then this is the book for you.

—Alvin Slaughter
Recording Artist and Inspirational Speaker
Founder, Alvin Slaughter International
www.alvinslaughter.com

INTRODUCTION

I have witnessed men, young and old, with great potential live unsuccessful lives. My desire is to see men become successful and fulfill their destinies in life. Often, this desire has burdened my heart. I have taught about it, preached about it, and now I am writing about it. If I can say or do something to empower *one man* to live in his God-ordained life, it would be worth it to me. However, I believe this book will be empowerment to men from many walks of life. Men, God wants to bless your life.

Sometimes as men, we are always told what needs to be done, but we are not quite sure how to execute with precision what needs to be done. I endeavor to give you principles that are applicable and useful to your everyday life. These principles will make you think, show you how to walk in a spirit of elevation, and enable you to become doers. Take these principles, meditate upon them, and share them with someone because they are sure to change your life.

While this book is directed to men, you will find portions speaking directly to women. I know women have a curious nature and will want to keep abreast of what is being imparted into the lives of their men. So gentlemen, you will find portions where I address women as well.

To the ladies reading, this book will bless you as well as your families. I believe your man will find many answers he has

14

been searching for. He will find the tools for empowerment that will affect his life spiritually, mentally, physically, financially and in every area possible. This gives you a reason to rejoice because if this impacts his life, it will certainly impact yours. I encourage you to send copies of this book to your son, brother, uncle or your father, so they can receive this life-changing book. It is one which can revolutionize and turn men around.

We need men of valor and worth who are ready to fulfill their divine destiny. God is searching, our women are longing, our families are crying, and the world is looking for real men in this 21st century.

—Bishop L. W. Francisco III

CHAPTER ONE

The Divinely Appointed Man

We are facing a dilemma in our society today that has gone unnoticed by many. It is a war that has been declared on the identities and destinies of today's men. Never in history have so many men lacked the understanding of their purpose in life. We live in a time where men are struggling to understand what it truly means to be a *real man*. Some men have settled for just being baby makers, but I want you to know you are more than that. You are a divinely appointed man. Inside of you is the ability to overcome the hurdles that have stopped you from forging a meaningful life. Inside of you is the power to overcome negative stereotypes and attitudes of our society. Certainly, we face unique challenges. It's a reality in the world we live in, but it's not a reality we cannot overcome. We can deal with all the things we face on a day-to-day basis when we understand our purpose and know why we are here on this earth.

From the beginning of time, God planted something unique inside of every man. Although we are not always fully aware of it, it's waiting to be discovered. God has planted tremendous potential inside of *you* and *me*. It is essential for us to understand this in order to fulfill our divine destiny. While our potential is a gift from God, it is a threat to the enemy. We are dangerous to the enemy when we understand our purpose and potential in life. Therefore, it is imperative to recognize that we are a threat to the devil. He hates a man who recognizes what God has deposited inside of him and knows *who he is* and *Whose he is.* You may not know the tremendous value God has placed inside of you—but He does! If you didn't know you had tremendous potential inside of you—*you do now!*

THE INFLUENCE OF MAN

There is something God has placed inside of us called "the seed of life." In essence, God refers to us as the progenitors of life. We are the givers of life. We are able to produce life in the physical and spiritual realm. We are the ones who actually make it happen. Without the male seed it's just not going to happen. The earth would eventually fade away. Therefore, we have an awesome responsibility to understand what satan has attempted to do since the beginning of time— destroy the male seed! We see this through the annals of history from the Garden of Eden to the struggles of Cain and Abel, to the attacks of Pharaoh and Herod, and even in our society today. There is an assault against the male. Satan understood if he could destroy the male seed, he could destroy the vehicle which causes life to be birthed. If he could destroy the male, then he could destroy the very creation of God. For that reason, we must recognize his schemes to keep us in the dark about our purpose, potential, and influence so that he can't destroy our lives.

We are also a threat to the enemy because we possess an inherit intergenerational power as a man. Intergenerational power is potent positive influence. You have influence you are not fully aware of. There is power inside of you that you need to tap into and recognize because you have the ability to affect generations—either positively or negatively. What an awesome revelation that we, as men, have the ability to affect generations to come. We are the hub, and everything in our God-assigned region revolves around us. Everything revolves around how we react, how we respond, how we identify, and how we participate in our activities. Every single thing—our children, our wives, our jobs, our settings, our circumstances, our churches—everything operates according to our temperament. Did you know you had this kind of potency, influence, and power? It's all there for you to make a difference in the world.

TAKING YOUR RIGHTFUL PLACE

"And I sought for a man among them, that should make up the hedge, and stand in the gap before me for the land, that I should not destroy it: but I found none" (Ezekiel 22:30). Here we find a little scripture predicate which speaks of God's search for man. We find the search for man is not a new thing; it's the same old thing. God has been looking for a long time. God looked in the Garden of Eden for Adam: *"And the LORD God called unto Adam, and said unto him, Where art thou?"* (Genesis 3:9). God looked in the Old Testament: *"And I sought for a man among them...but I found none."* God is still looking for a man today. Why has God been looking for a man? God is looking for a man who won't be ashamed to find out what it really means to be a real man and is willing to position himself to be used by Him. God is simply looking for men who will rise and take their rightful place. God is still looking today.

When we don't understand and walk in our purpose then we leave the doorway open for confusion and chaos to enter our lives. If the enemy can come through the door of confusion then all types of things will be birthed out of sync and out of harmony of God's plan. The enemy works on a man's psyche and on a man's ego to make him feel like he has to prove himself. He makes him feel that he has to be macho, on top or the head, so he can work to destroy him. If the enemy can keep us full of chaos, confusion, strife, and stress then he can keep us in a position where we are reproducing negativity. If we get in this position then he's winning the battle against the male seed. If we are in our rightful place then he doesn't have the ability to create chaos and confusion in our lives.

If we are going to have order in our homes, in our society, in our nation and world, it's going to come through men who have taken their rightful place. When men are "out of order," children become rebellious and women begin to lead (Isaiah 3:12). There is nothing wrong with a woman in leadership, nonetheless, we know God's divine authority mandates men to provide the oversight for their household and take initiative to bear the responsibility. As men of divine destiny, we have to learn to walk in the wisdom of God and in the knowledge of who we are in the Lord. I'm going to keep reminding you that we are the anointed progenitors, we are the anointed givers of life, and we are God's seed whereby we recreate life. We recreate what God has planted in us and we are anointed by God to reproduce. The challenge for many of us is learning how to protect our seed. We must learn how to protect our anointing, because we know the devil wants to destroy our ability to create and cultivate what God has entrusted to us.

There are things inside of me that God has entrusted me with that the enemy doesn't want me to birth and give life to. What is inside of you that has a battle going on in your life? Man, look at yourself in the mirror and recognize that's what you're going to reproduce—not just what you physically look like, but what's in your heart—what's inside of you. I want to ask you a couple of questions: "What is in your spirit, man? What is flowing out of your moral and spiritual value system?" Because that's the thing we have to be mindful of as men. Not only do we carry the seed of life, but we carry the seed of life to create images that will look like us. The images will have our nature. I want to challenge you in this book to look at yourself in this respect. When we are operating in divine destiny then everything we touch will be blessed. If we can get in our spirit that God desires for us to be reproducers of abundant life and wants to do some awesome things in our lives, then we can get in our spirit that God wants to use each one of us, and no man is inferior.

WE CAN WIN!

We can win this war! As a matter of fact, we already have through Jesus Christ. We just have to recognize the times we are living in and understand our purpose and take a stand. God, our wives, and our children are all looking for real men who will stand in their rightful position. They are looking for men who will allow divine authority to flow through their lives. When men don't take their rightful places, the complete order of humanity is thrown out of sync. When we do take our rightful place as men, we usher in the move of God. God is looking so that He can cause destiny of this life or humanity to be fulfilled. So, it's important brothers, to realize God has a plan for our lives. God wants every man blessed out of his socks. He wants you to be able to give life and not just any kind of life but God wants you to be able to give productive life. We must never forget God is on our side. *"...if God be for us who can be against us?"* (Romans 8:31).

While the devil loves a man who feels he is just a baby maker, he hates a man who understands his rightful place in society. It's reality—we are hated by the enemy, but a greater reality is, we are loved by the Almighty God Who has called us to excel in life and make a difference. Yes, we are at war for our identities and our destinies, but we must raise the standard. We must fight to provide a Godly example for our sons and their sons. God is looking for men who can stand up and say, "I am willing to be the one who will make a difference. I am willing to be the one who won't succumb to the pressures of society. I am willing to be the one who will stand by my home and take care of my family." God is looking for men who are willing to equip themselves to deal with the enemy, society, and changing times.

CHAPTER TWO

Times Have Changed

As I think about the society we live in, I realize we are challenged in our male and female relationships in this twenty-first century. Things have definitely changed over the course of time. Relationships which were prevalent in our parents' generation have taken a paradigm shift. We no longer have the type of family structure that prevailed fifty years ago. I've come to the realization that families and relationships are not the same as they used to be.

Fifty years ago, most households were supported by the man of the house. The man provided for the main stay of the home while the wife stayed home to manage the household affairs. Now, the script has been flipped! Most women have jobs outside of the home and work just as hard as a man. The lives of men have been deeply impacted by the shift from an industrial age (assembly line/production worker) to an information age (technology computer based society). Households have been impacted by empowered women joining the workforce and by new patterns of values and changing family dynamics.

HUMAN OR WHO-MAN

In this twenty-first century, we seem to have entered into an age of male insecurities and confusion. There was a study done in 2005 that explored the state of masculinity in the workplace. Two-thousand men were interviewed and the study showed 50% of men in the United States and 64% of men in Europe are unclear of their role in society and really don't know where they fit in. They just don't know exactly where their place is anymore. I believe it's simply because we've come from a time that has quickly evolved from an industrial age to an information age.

Fifty years ago, men could identify their place in society. Men were able to define their masculinity based on their brawn and ability to produce in the manufacturing industry. Men were the producers and women were the keepers of the home. Due to the transition from an industrial age to an information age, we now have women who are just as smart as men and maybe a little smarter. If the truth be told, women think a little faster than men. This is a challenge to us! For example, if a married couple is having a dispute, the man may be on point A, but the woman has already covered points E, F and G. The woman may seem to be light years ahead of the man. While he is still trying to remember what he was *going to say,* she has *already said it.* Don't get upset, gentlemen. God has given women a unique ability to think and recall very quickly.

We must come to grips with the fact that we live in a society where women have entered into the workforce which was once considered taboo. In the late 1950's there was a popular family television show called *Leave it to Beaver.* (I must be telling my age now.) The family was called the Cleavers. The husband's name was Ward and the wife's name was June. They had two sons, Wally and Beaver (some of you remember). This show painted a vivid picture of what people thought the ideal household looked like years ago. Back then, June needed the financial securities Ward had to offer. She needed him to take care of the mortgage, utilities, automobile payment, buy groceries, etc.

In the 1980's, another family-oriented television sitcom was created called *The Cosby Show*. The family was known by the name Huxtable. They were an upper-middle class family who lived in Brooklyn, New York. The Huxtables consisted of the husband, Cliff; the wife, Clair; and their five children: Sondra, Denise, Theodore, Vanessa, and Rudy. When we began to watch *The Cosby Show* we found that Cliff and Clair both held jobs. They were both professionals. Cliff was an obstetrician and Clair was an attorney. They were both educated. The whole dynamic chain of mutual reciprocity was evident in their relationship. I mention these television shows because it brings reality home. Our women are no longer at home waiting on men and living dependent lives. They are in the workforce achieving and excelling, just like men. Today's women understand, in order for them to do what they have to do, they need a real man. They need men who understand who they are.

My purpose for writing this, is not to bash men, but simply to identify the dilemma we are facing in our society. I entitled this portion of the chapter "Human or Who-man" because I believe we need to revisit *the who*. *Who are we as men?* What is our function? What is our purpose? What has God assigned us to do? For the reality is, gentlemen, until we can define our masculinity, we are simply frightened little boys in grown men's bodies. Until you can define who you are and know what God has called you to be with confidence, your masculinity will be undefined. You will become one of the 50% who are frightened little boys in grown men's bodies, trying to function in a grown-up world with a little boy's mentality. It is scary to be a grown man and not have a mind mature enough to understand who you are. You are more than human. You are a man, and you must be able to define yourself beyond your humanity.

A NOTICE TO LADIES

Be careful that you don't fall into the category of being in a relationship with an insecure or confused man. I want to remind you of the statistics which stated 50% of men in the United States are insecure or confused. I teach this because I want my daughters and your daughters to understand they don't want to become involved in a relationship based on good looks. The man may have a good game, but he may not be able to finish the game. A real woman must understand that a real man can define his masculinity. If you connect with a little boy in a grown man's body you simply become a surrogate mother figure. If you become a surrogate mother figure, you will literally walk around your own house on eggshells trying to protect your husband's ego. Ladies, if this happens, instead of only raising your children, you'll have to raise him.

WHERE IS THE MAN?

I have attempted to build a foundation of what I believe we are facing today which is a shortage of men who really know how to define themselves. The statistics I shared with you reveal the condition of most of today's men. These men who are trying to discover who they are, whose they are and where they belong are trying to discover where they fit. Strong powerful women intimidate many of these men, and they don't know what to do. So, they begin to relegate themselves into different areas of life. There are four categories of defining male men. Each one of these men need a different type of woman. I want to share the four types of men the survey listed:

1. The Metro Man

The metro man is a man who has adopted more feminine traits. He is a man in touch with his feminine side more than other men are. The metro man has the tendency to spend a lot of extra time in the bathroom and in front of mirrors. He may even have more lotions, moisturizers, and creams than most women. The metro man is sensitive and in touch with his emotional realm. He has the tendency to identify well with the feelings of a woman. He is not afraid to cry, like most men are. He will let the tears flow.

I am not making fun of the metro man. However, I want you to understand, God knew there would be men who would try to get in touch with their feminine side. He knew from the beginning Adam might have a problem with trying to get in touch with his feminine side. But, if you go back to Genesis, God knew He had to fix this thing before it got out of hand. So what did God do? The Bible says, *"...the LORD God caused a deep sleep to fall upon Adam, and he slept: and he took one of his ribs"* (Genesis 2:21). In essence, He reached inside of man and took the rib out. It was like He was saying, "I'm going to take all the femininity out of man." Or in other words, I'm taking the woman out of you. I'm going to create a separate entity and I will call her Woman. I believe God took all the femininity out of man in the beginning.

2. The Retro Man

This man is entrenched in the typical male old school behavior. He's the retro man who is an old school brother. What is an old school brother? He is the one who doesn't see his wife or women as equals. He sees women as subordinates and second class. The retro man is the man who says, "I am the top dog and that's the way it is. I don't care if you like it because I run stuff around here!" He believes in running everything. He loves being in control. When this man comes home, everybody in his household goes to their room because no one wants to be around him. The retro man believes his home is "his kingdom" and "he rules." When he says jump, he expects his woman to say, "How high?" There are not too many of these around anymore. Today's woman isn't having it which is causing this breed to die out quickly.

3. The Patriarch

The patriarch is the fatherly figure. He is the nurturer of the family. This man thrives on being able to provide for his family. His primary focus is how he can care for his family. His primary thrust is not his personal gain but making everyone else in his household feel good about themselves.

4. The Power Seeker

The power seeker's personal motivation is his career. This man is very concerned about his image. He loves to give the impression of being powerful, but hates to show signs of weakness. Even if he doesn't have the ability to do something, he wants people to think he does. He's about money, prestige, position and power. If he doesn't have money, prestige, position and power, he will fake like he has all of these. The power seeking man's life centers around himself.

The metros, retros, patriarchs, and power seekers all need a particular type of woman. They need a woman who defines her value and worth through the man. If she defines her value and worth through the man, she will either bow down to the man or dominate the man. Her sense of accomplishment is found in either acquiescing or domineering. The only way you can live with a metro, retro, patriarch, or power seeker is either you have to take a subservient role or you control everything.

Women have traditionally taken a subordinate role trying to fit into the constraint of developing a relationship with a metro man, retro man, patriarch or a power seeker. They have diminished their capacity to try to be in relationship with these types of men. That's why one woman can't evaluate her relationship with a man based on another woman's perception. Why? You don't know what type of man she is involved with. While one woman may have a metro man or a retro man, she may be advising you on how to deal with a metro man and you may have a patriarch or a power seeker. So, it's hard to compare apples to apples because you're not quite sure what kind of man you are dealing with. The challenge from the woman's perception is understanding what kind of man she is working with. What is a woman to do? Is she to deny her value and worth to settle? Or is she to become the woman God is calling her to be?

WHAT IS A REAL MAN?

The fifth category I would like to add to the above definition is what I call a *real man*. We've got the metro man, the retro man, the patriarch, and the power seeker, but I want to speak from the perspective of the *real man.* I asked the question before, What kind of man does a real woman need? The answer is: A real woman needs a real man. Here is my description of a real man:

> He is powerful, yet passionate. He is dominating, but not overbearing. He controls his anger and is never violent. He is decisive, but he is not a dictator. He knows what he has to do and does it with excellence. He is fun, but he is not a fool. He is a provider and protector, but never a slacker. He is up to a challenge; it inspires him. He's willing to take the hit and stand alone if necessary. He's not a whiner, but a winner.

> If a woman is walking down the street and the man pushes her to save himself—*he's not a real man*. There is something about when a real man shows up. A real man will make chills run down a woman's spine. A real man will make her just shine. When a real man shows up peace prevails.

A REAL WOMAN NEEDS A REAL MAN

Since we've identified the characteristics of a *real man,* we will now turn our attention to defining what a *real woman* is. Of course, if a *real woman* needs a *real man* then a *real man* needs a *real woman*. Some of you may already think you have a Proverbs 31 wife. Some of you may think you don't, but in reality, you do. The challenge may not be her, it might be you. Proverbs 31:10 says, *"...who can find a virtuous woman?"* Who can find her? I would like to expand on this passage of Scripture and raise another question, besides the one we are used to hearing, and ask: who can handle a virtuous woman? Who can deal with a virtuous woman? Who can handle the power she brings? Who can handle the authority which she possesses?

A MOTHER'S ADVICE TO HER SON

Who can find a virtuous woman? for her price is far above rubies.

The heart of her husband doth safely trust in her, so that he shall have no need of spoil.

She will do him good and not evil all the days of her life.

She seeketh wool, and flax, and worketh willingly with her hands.

She is like the merchants' ships; she bringeth her food from afar.

She riseth also while it is yet night, and giveth meat to her household, and a portion to her maidens.

She considereth a field, and buyeth it: with the fruit of her hands she planteth a vineyard.

She girdeth her loins with strength, and strengtheneth her arms.

She perceiveth that her merchandise is good: her candle goeth not out by night.

She layeth her hands to the spindle, and her hands hold the distaff.

She stretcheth out her hand to the poor; yea, she reacheth forth her hands to the needy.

She is not afraid of the snow for her household: for all her household are clothed with scarlet.

She maketh herself coverings of tapestry; her clothing is silk and purple.

Her husband is known in the gates, when he sitteth among the elders of the land.

She maketh fine linen, and selleth it; and

delivereth girdles unto the merchant.

Strength and honour are her clothing; and she shall rejoice in time to come.

She openeth her mouth with wisdom; and in her tongue is the law of kindness.

She looketh well to the ways of her household, and eateth not the bread of idleness.

Her children arise up, and call her blessed; her husband also, and he praiseth her.

Many daughters have done virtuously, but thou excellest them all.

Favour is deceitful, and beauty is vain: but a woman that feareth the LORD, she shall be praised.

Give her of the fruit of her hands; and let her own works praise her in the gates.

—Proverbs 31:10-31

As we examine this passage of scripture we find it was not necessarily penned for women to measure up to a particular mark. It was a mother instructing her son on what type of woman he needed to secure in his life—*a real woman*. You must understand what Solomon's mother was saying to her son. She was sharing with Solomon that he shouldn't be intimidated by a real woman. When she began to instruct him and identify certain traits the woman in his life should have, she challenges him with the question, *"who can find a virtuous woman?"* Once again I ask, "Who can handle a virtuous woman?" Solomon's mother wanted him to understand the question was not *who can find* her but rather *who can handle* a strong, focused, self-sufficient woman! Not only did she challenge him but she challenges many of us today. The kind of woman she was talking about is not necessarily how we view them today. She described an assertive, independent woman, who was able to take care of herself.

The sad reality is, the average man in the twenty-first century would be insecure and intimidated by this woman. He would be utterly unable to cope with her. The average man in the twenty-first century would not be able to deal with a woman who gets up early in the morning and takes care of her house. He would not be able to deal with a woman who is preparing the meals and going out to buy a field. He would not be able to handle her having her own business with no consultation from him. The twenty-first century man would have a problem with a woman with this great magnitude of strength. Yes, the twenty-first century man would struggle knowing his woman was an entrepreneur, humanitarian, administrator, counselor, protector, provider, communicator, and mother, who is able to handle *all* of her business proficiently without his assistance. The average man would not be able to handle this kind of woman because she is such a strong, self-sufficient and influential woman with her own money. This woman doesn't have to ask her husband, "Can I have some money to get my nails done?" Why? She is buying land, merchandise, and handling her businesses. The average twenty-first century man would be very intimidated and shaking in his boots by this woman.

My endeavor here is to help men understand that as brothers we don't have to be intimidated by strong women. It is an old paradigm which has generated from ages that has made men feel discomforted by strong women. I want you to notice the husband's position in the above passage of Scripture. The Bible says, *"...The heart of her husband doth safely trust in her...he calls her blessed."* In essence, he's telling his wife, "Baby, go get it! Handle your business, do whatever you have to do, because we are in this thing together." Gentlemen, whenever your wife is blessed—*you are blessed!* I feel this way concerning my wife. If she's blessed, I'm blessed and I'm not intimidated.

The Bible says, *"Her husband is known in the gates, when he sitteth among the elders of the land."* How do you think he can afford to sit at the gates with the elders? He can sit at the gates with the elders because he has a virtuous woman handling business. With a wife like this, there is no need to worry whether or not the electricity bill or the mortgage will be paid. Instead of this man being intimidated by the woman God blessed him with, he embraces her. The husband who is keenly aware of his wife's power and abilities will use his authority to release and cover her. I know that's a challenge for us as men. This woman made a decision to break status quo and decided to make a difference. Men, we need real women like this in our lives who are willing to make a difference.

THE DEMAND FOR POTENTIAL

The bottom line is, a "real man" needs a "real woman" and a "real woman" needs a man who doesn't need to be pacified. She needs a man who doesn't need to be primped or cuddled. A real woman needs a real man who is not afraid to recognize her gifts and see her as a facilitator who will draw out the best in him. Some of you may be asking, "What's wrong with men today?" "Why aren't there more *real men* today?" I pose another question to you, "What's wrong with our women today?" What's wrong with a woman who will hook up with a man who won't work? What's wrong with a woman who won't make a demand on the man's potential?

Real men are motivated when a demand is placed on their potential. When a demand is made on my potential, that's when I shine the best. When I am put in a difficult situation, that's when I really stand up. I don't go run and hide. When you put me in a difficult situation that's when I get my most creative juices and flow in what I am called to do. The problem we have in our society today is, real women have connected with men, but refuse to place a demand on the man's potential. So, the man acquiesces and backs down and won't do what he's assigned to do. Once a demand is placed on *a real man's* potential, he will bring to pass what needs to be fulfilled.

I would like to talk about the two women who have challenged me the most in my life. I wasn't allowed to punk out, quit, run, hide, or take the easy road. We must face our demons, fears, and challenges. Not only must we face them but we must deal with them. God knew who to call to help us face them—real women! Real men are not intimidated and recognize a real woman is a valuable asset. He respects what she brings to the table and thanks God for the gift he has been given. I would not be where I am today, if my wife and mother hadn't pushed me.

MY WIFE

The average man could not handle being married to a woman like my wife. While other men's wives may pump them up, my wife challenges me. I would have failed pre-marital counseling and never passed the test to be able to marry my wife. She made a demand on my potential. When I first started preaching, I would preach up a storm and feel extremely confident, until the ride home. When I got in the car I expected my wife to shower me with accolades and tell me how good I preached. I waited for her to stroke my ego and tell me how great I was. Instead, she would ask, "How do you spell that word you used today?" Needless to say, my feelings would be hurt. I felt like asking her, "That's all you can come up with? You can't tell me how good I was?" All I got was, "How do you spell that word you used today?" I didn't fall, crack, or let her see me shudder. My wife's response caused me to grow and go to new levels. It caused me to open the dictionary and start learning new words. It caused me to study a little harder and become a little more proficient. It made me sharpen my edge. She actually did me a favor by not sitting there telling me in the middle of my brokenness how good I was, when I really wasn't. She refused to lie to me. She challenged me to pull out what was inside of me, so I could become all that God called me to be.

I've learned from my wife to step up to the plate when she places a demand on my potential. I understand now, as a *real man,* I don't have to be intimidated by her strength, power, or intelligence. I embrace these wonderful attributes she possesses. The reality is, whatever she does—I can do! So, I support my wife and tell her to pursue her dreams, and I push her as she pushes me.

MY MOTHER

When you have a real woman, she won't pacify you. I grew up in a house with a real woman—my mother. My mother used to tell me, "Boy, your wife is going to love me. I'm not going to raise a punk or a pansy; you are going to be a real man. You are going to know how to take care of a woman. Your wife is going to love me because I am going to raise you right." I didn't have the luxury of being raised in a home where a child could get away with stuff. If I cut the grass wrong I had to cut it over again. If I didn't cut the grass when I was supposed to cut it, I had to cut it in the rain, even in a thunderstorm. It really didn't matter. I had to do what my parents told me to do.

I remember my dad's garden. It was his, yet it seemed as

though it was mine. I remember the boys in the neighborhood laughing at me. We had a giant backyard which almost looked like a farm. My responsibilities were to pull weeds, plant corn, hoe beans, cut okra, pick string beans, and shuck corn. When my father would say, "Look at my garden!" I often wanted to ask, "What are you talking about your garden?" I wanted to smack him into reality. I felt he didn't have a garden because I did all the work! It didn't matter if I had homework or extracurricular activities. My being on the football team didn't excuse me from work. My mother made sure I knew there was no excuse for not taking care of my duties at home.

TO ALL THE MOTHERS

Mothers, if you're going to raise a *real man*, the time to begin is *now*! Don't cut any slack on your young men. Make them cut the grass, wash dishes, empty the trash, make their beds, and clean their rooms. Make your boys do things that will make real men out of them. I grew up in a house with two brothers and no sisters. Therefore, I had to wash dishes. I tried to be smart when I washed them so I would leave them a little greasy in hopes that Momma wouldn't ask me to wash them anymore. My mother being the momma she was would come through and rub her finger on them and say, "Uh-huh!" She would dump all of them back, even the clean ones. She would tell me to wash them again. I was obedient and never challenged my mother. Because of this I believe my mother raised a real man.

Remember, mothers, you want to raise a man who can handle something. You want to raise real men who can connect with real women so when a woman begins to place a demand on his potential, he won't crumble. He will step up and become stronger. A man who has a real woman, who makes a demand on his potential, won't run and be scared of her. You won't be intimidated by her; instead, you will be challenged by her and say, "I can do it too!" As a man, you need to be able to say, "I may not know how to do it now but I can figure it out."

TAKE YOUR STAND

The sad reality is, in homes today, we've got real women with men who aren't real and real men with women who aren't real. A real man recognizes the strength in his woman and doesn't want her to bow down and diminish her capacity just to live with him. Most women have to bring it down about a thousand just to be at peace in their own home. A woman's mind is always ticking and her brain continually processing incoming thoughts. Your woman can see stuff that needs to be done but she knows if she says anything to you, you will fall all to pieces because you can't handle it. She also knows she can't challenge you; if she makes a demand on your potential, you'll start whining and crumbling. But, a real woman understands she has to place a demand on her man's potential.

Sisters, the light bulb will never shine until you turn the light switch on. A real woman needs a real man who understands her value and her worth. Sisters, never let any man define you. I teach my three daughters not to let a man define their value or worth. A real man will respect your power, your intelligence, and will embrace your authority. He doesn't need you to act less intelligent to make him feel good about himself. He needs you to stand up and turn on the light switch of potential in his life. He needs you to stand up and challenge him to become everything God has assigned him to be. Take your stand!

CHAPTER THREE

Submission or Subjection?

There is a subject I feel we need to have a clearer understanding of as *real men*. It is the subject of submission and subjection. In our western culture, it has become a very sensitive subject. Many people misunderstand this matter because it has been defined in a western context. We've used our human understanding rather than our spiritual understanding. In Christendom it has been used to guide the behavior patterns of women (especially married women) on how they should conduct themselves in relationship to their husbands. I want to deal with this subject matter by examining Ephesians 5:21-33 in *The Message Bible*:

> Out of respect for Christ, be courteously reverent to one another. Wives, understand and support your husbands in ways that show your support for Christ. The husband provides leadership to his wife the way Christ does to his church, not by domineering but by cherishing. So just as the church submits to Christ as he exercises such leadership, wives should likewise submit to their husbands.
>
> Husbands, go all out in your love for your wives, exactly as Christ did for the church—a love marked by giving, not getting. Christ's love makes the church

whole. His words evoke her beauty. Everything He does and says is designed to bring the best out of her, dressing her in dazzling white silk, radiant with holiness. And that is how husbands ought to love their wives. They're really doing themselves a favor—since they're already "one" in marriage.

No one abuses his own body, does he? No, he feeds and pampers it. That's how Christ treats us, the church, since we are part of His body. And this is why a man leaves father and mother and cherishes his wife. No longer two, they become "one flesh." This is a huge mystery, and I don't pretend to understand it all. What is clearest to me is the way Christ treats the church. And this provides a good picture of how each husband is to treat his wife, loving himself in loving her, and how each wife is to honor her husband.

This portion of Scripture supports the typical theme of female inferiority and male domination, if it is taken out of its context. Of course, this is the retro man's favorite Scripture as long as it's out of context. In the context this is usually understood, it places a female in a lower status or a lower category than a male. Because of the way it has been misunderstood many women have been relegated to coming under their husband's authority, losing their opinion and ability to speak rationally even in their own household.

A LITTLE HISTORY

For centuries the Bible has been used as a tool to manipulate and condone the actions of those who benefit the most from it, meaning: Power brokers have taken the Scriptures from its inception to control people. History mandates and dictates to us and reveals how individuals have basically taken the

Bible and utilized it as a tool of manipulation. They use it in order to gain power over individuals or even a group of people. The Sanhedrin who were a group consisting of Pharisees and Sadducees used the early scriptural text to control and become elitist. If you didn't pray and fast often, or go to the synagogue regularly, or follow the Mosaic laws as they did, then you didn't fit into their group. They used and abused the Word of God to benefit themselves and make themselves look good. Not only them, the twelfth-thirteenth century church used the Word of God to initiate crusades where they tried to force people into their version of Christianity. They used God's Word to justify pillage, rape, and killing. It was basically used as a power mechanism to justify their own private agendas. Traveling through the centuries, we find the colonists who justified slavery by using the Word of God for their benefit. They used the Word of God to support their views of slavery using the Scripture that *"slaves were to be obedient to their masters."* It justified their views on slavery. All of these are examples of people who considered themselves doing "the bidding of the Lord," but they didn't flip to tell the other side. Once again, we see the Word being used as a tool of manipulation and control!

In the early twentieth century, it was used as a tool to manipulate women. Basically, they were kept in a position where they couldn't vote and didn't have rights. They were considered second class citizens. The Bible was used to deny women access to many things. Even today, cults are created to manipulate people with a tool that was intended to liberate people. The Bible was never intended to be used as a wedge to hit you over the head. It wasn't meant to be used as a tool to gain control over you.

Before we go any further, I just want you to understand a little bit of the historical data and chronological order of how the Bible has been used as a tool to control. I want you to be aware of how it has been used as a tool of manipulation to benefit certain individuals, even though the intent of the Bible was never meant to hold anyone captive, but to liberate them. The Bible says in John 10:10, *"The thief cometh not, but for to steal, and to kill, and to destroy: I am come that they might have life, and that they might have it more abundantly."*

THE MISSING PIECE

"Wherefore the law was our schoolmaster to bring us unto Christ, that we might be justified by faith. But after that faith is come, we are no longer under a schoolmaster" (Galatians 3:24-25). The law was designed to point you in the right direction. Once you arrived, the law was no longer needed. In essence, Apostle Paul was saying, there is no need to mandate or to dictate to you anymore. He further clarifies this when he wrote: *"For ye are all the children of God by faith in Christ Jesus. For as many of you as have been baptized into Christ have put on Christ"* (Galatians 3:26-27). Once you come into a relationship with Christ, once you are baptized in Him then something supernatural takes place; something changes and shifts and moves in the spirit. Here is the piece that is not taught much or fully understood: Once you are baptized in Christ, *"...there is neither Jew nor Greek, there is neither bond nor free, there is neither male nor female: for ye are all one in Christ Jesus"* (Galatians 3:28). I know that it has been preached that there is a divide, but Paul wrote to the Galatians and told them there is no divide for those who are in Christ. For once we come "in Christ" there is no Jew, Greek, or Gentile; there is no bond or free, no male or female, in Christ we are one.

SUBJECTION

Subjection is a powerful word, but like I said before, it has been misunderstood. As I was preparing to speak at one of our women's conferences, the Lord spoke to my heart and said, "I want you to tell the truth about subjection because in the last days I'm pouring out my spirit on all flesh. I really can't do what I desire to do as long as people are bound by traditions and don't really understand what I said. They have been bound by what people have said from generations past and they really haven't gotten into My Word to understand and rightfully divide the Word of Truth for themselves. What I am saying to the church today is, I want them to rightfully divide truth."

I have a mandate on me to share this message with the Body of Christ, especially men. If I am perfectly honest with you, this area was once hard for me also. I will be the first to admit, I was one of the ones who said to my wife, *"You are suppose to submit!"* (I didn't say she did. I'm just saying, I was one of the ones who said it.)

From a biblical perspective, the word submission and subjection are synonymous. It is the Greek word *hupothaso* and it means to submit one's self unto. Therefore, subjection and submission means to submit yourself unto, but we have not taken this text and defined it in a biblical context today. In the book of Ephesians it says the wife should be subject to her husband, but the *Webster's* dictionary defines subjection this way: "one that is placed under the authority or control, one who holds allegiance to the power or dominion of another, to force to undergo or to endure something unpleasant." If we use our western definition to understand the theological perspective, we can see how quickly things can be taken out of context.

When Apostle Paul wrote his letter to the Ephesians, he included a very informative section on submission (Ephesians 5:21). The submission Paul was referring to was to be demonstrated to one another in the fear, or in the reverence, or in the respect of God. Paul's letter (which is known to us today as Scripture) does not support power or dominance over another, neither does it indicate there has to be compliance by the female because of male dominance. He gave clarification when he stated that subjection works when we submit one to another out of respect for God. That is the basis by which this concept or theological perception is written. Nevertheless, this text has been preached that man is over and woman is less than for years.

Many men, one way or another, seem to miss Ephesians 5:21 and the only verse of Scripture they see or hear is Ephesians 5:22 which says, *"...wives submit to your husbands."* They want to completely wipe verse twenty-one out of the Bible and forget it was ever written. They want their wives to be submissive, recognize them as the head, and realize that's just the way it is. That's all they believe and hear. Some may not agree with me because while growing up, they have been taught the wife can't do anything unless she first submits to her husband. The reality is, we shouldn't be able to do anymore than the wife. In no way does this Scripture infer that a woman is a second class citizen or of lesser value than a man. It simply defines function and responsibility.

I want you to have a clearer understanding of the type of subjection God is talking about. It is a reciprocal agreement between husband and wife. It is not a lopsided, one-sided submission. This mutual agreement between husband and wife simply states that out of reverence for God we will respect one other. So it doesn't mean, "Woman, shut up,

I'm the head of this house!" or "Woman, what did I tell you to do?" Nor is the woman to tell the man, "Shut up, I'm in charge" or "Sit down, you don't know what you're talking about."No, go back to verse twenty-one, which says *"submitting yourself one to another."* Please keep in mind, we don't necessarily submit because it's the right or wrong thing to do or because we want to, but submitting one to another is always to be done out of respect for God.

THE AMAZING POWER OF LOVE

"For the husband is the head of the wife, even as Christ is the head of the church: and he is the saviour of the body. Therefore as the church is subject unto Christ, so let the wives be to their own husbands in every thing" (Ephesians 5:23-24). After sharing this passage of Scripture with my congregation during one of my sermons, I shared another way I felt this passage of Scripture could read: "For the husband is responsible for the wife, even as Christ is responsible for the church" (Francisco Translation). After sharing this, I asked the following questions: "Why does the church submit to Christ? Why do we, as a body of believers, submit to the Lord? Why do we submit to the Sovereignty of Jesus and bow at His feet? Why do we worship Him, bless Him and praise Him? What sets Jesus apart from Mohammad, Buddha, Confucius, Hare Krishna or any other icon?" We answered the questions and came to the conclusion: The church submits to Christ because He gave Himself for the church.

We don't say *yes* to Jesus because He told us to say *yes* nor because it's just the right thing to do. We say *yes* to Jesus because He gave Himself for the Church. He endured the punishment, the agony, the pain, the rejection, the beatings, the misunderstandings, and the Cross. We find the answer to our *why* in John 3:16, which states: *"For God so loved the world that he gave his only begotten Son..."* Jesus came into the world and gave His life because He loved you, me and everyone else who would come before and after us. He loved us enough to go to the Cross and say, *"Not my will, but Father your will be done."* Jesus loved us as God's creation more than He loved His own life.

Love does something amazing. Love says, "I do this *in spite of,* not *because of.*" I will break this down some more for you. Love is not a feeling. Love is not a sensation. Love is not a passing whim. Love is not something we fall in and out of. We can fall "in like" and "out of like" but love is consistent. Love doesn't change. Here is the amazing thing, when we truly follow the example of Jesus, we understand God's way of submission or subjection. In other words, God is saying to the husband, follow My Son's example and provide for your wife in the same way. Your ultimate goal should never be what you can get out of your wife; it should be to love her *in spite* of and not *because of.* If you love your wife for her gorgeous shape, understand that, in time, that too will pass away. Love is a "many-splendored" thing but you must understand love has a price attached to it. Love means I will always be here for you no matter what happens or transpires. Isn't that what Jesus did for us?

Jesus' attitude and actions were always "even though." Even though you hate Me—*I still love you!* Even though you beat Me and nail Me to the Cross—*I still love you!* Even today, when we distance ourselves from Him, deny Him, or reject Him—*He still loves us!* Love says, "I put my life on the line." Once you know Jesus loves you this much, you have no problem bowing at His feet. And you have no problem calling Him, Lord.

THE CHRIST OF THE HOME

"Husbands, love your wives, even as Christ also loved the church, and gave himself for it" (Ephesians 5:23). What I am simply encouraging you as a man to realize is that you are assigned by God as the head of your house to love your wife in spite of. If she never gives anything back to you, you are still called by God to be the Christ of your home. Husbands, when your wife knows you will put your *all* on the line *in spite of*, she has no problem saying, "You are the man!" It is not enough to say, "I'm the man." It must be evident in your daily walk and demonstrated in every thing you do. It has to show up that you love your wife just as Christ loved the Church. God has designed the husband and wife relationship as a mirror which reflects the relationship of Christ and the church. If the husband is the head, then the husband must be willing to endure the punishment, the agony, the pain, the rejection, the misunderstandings, and the Cross just as Christ did. The reason must be *not because* of, but *in spite of,* because he chooses to love. Christ gave Himself for the church because He loves the church. You must remember this gentlemen: You, as a husband, are the head of the wife not for what you can get out of her, but because of your love for her. So, you do what you do even when your wife doesn't perform or respond the way you feel she should. You are the Christ of your home when you reflect the image of Christ's love for the church.

THE 20th CENTURY WOMAN VS. THE 21st CENTURY WOMAN

We have been talking about subjection, but now I want to deal with submission for a moment. The word submission means to yield one's self to governance or authority, to defer or consent. I want you to recognize submission is vastly different from subjection in our western culture understanding. Remember the word subjection meant to be placed under authority or control of. A king has subjects who don't have a choice in the matter. They do what he says, when he says and how he says it. The word *subject* in our understanding is to be placed under, to be put under, to be placed there. But *submission* means to yield. Yield means *I choose* to acquiesce to the authority or the governance that's in my life. It doesn't mean you come and make me do anything or try to put me under.

The 21st century woman hasn't changed the paradigm of the theological context of the Scripture. She has simply challenged and forced us to refine and to distill it back into its original intent of reciprocity and balance. You must understand, this is not a feminist movement, however; it is a movement that is driving us back into the Scriptures for its original intent. This movement is taking us back where we can ask the questions: What does it really say? Did it really say what they said it says, or is it saying something differently? I submit to you, the challenge today is, the church is being pushed at all edges of the envelope to revisit Scripture to see what It's really saying.

You must understand the 21st century woman doesn't need a man to pay her bills or even to take care of her. For the most part, she's able to take care of herself. So, in order for her to submit, she needs a real man. In order for my wife to say, "I will yield to your governance or to your authority in my life," I've got to bring something to the table. I've got to give her something to work with. As the young men say, "Are you feeling me?"

I was looking around my neighborhood one day when I noticed my neighbor's wife cutting their grass. When I saw this, I began to think of the message she was sending to her husband. She was basically telling her husband, "If you won't cut it—I will! I don't need you to take care of me because I can take care of myself." Men, like I said before, we've got to bring something to the table. The 21st century woman and your mother are two different types of women. In order for the 21st century woman to submit and yield, you can't place her under anything. She will rise up and say, "Whoa, slow your roll!" and you will find yourself in an awkward situation looking real cheap. You will be looking cheap because you know it worked for your daddy, but it isn't working for you. Your daddy may have been able to speak to your momma and she would immediately execute his command. Your daddy may have been able to sit in his favorite chair while momma served him his dinner (while the rest of the family was at the table). But now, the 21st century woman says, "If you don't come and get it, *you will starve!*" Or "if you don't get up from your seat and fix your own plate, then you won't eat." Or "you better be thankful I cooked you something!" Your daddy may have been able to get away with this, but you can't.

I've struggled with it myself because I couldn't understand it. My daddy was the breadwinner. My momma took care of daddy and that was just the way it was. This was my perception and I expected the same thing in my relationship. When my daddy came home everyone knew the routine. Daddy would head to his favorite recliner where he'd remove his shoes. We immediately picked his shoes up and took them to his room. My dad would put his feet up while one of us got him a glass of iced tea. The other brought him his TV tray while someone else fixed his plate. Nobody messed with my daddy because daddy ran the house. Daddy took care of business and momma took care of daddy and the house.

I want to tell young men especially between the ages of 22 and 26, don't try to imitate what you see on television. Don't expect the way your daddy talked to your momma to work the same way for you because you might be in for a big surprise.

Remember what I shared with you earlier about the difference between the two television shows. There is a vast difference between June Cleaver in the late 1950's *Leave it to Beaver* television show and Clair Huxtable in the 1980's sitcom called *The Cosby Show*. We are not finding too many Junes today for they are becoming extinct. We are finding more Clair Huxtables who are able to lead independent lives if they choose to. They are able to contribute to the table of life just like we are (some are able to bring more). We must be aware that the dynamics are changing at a very fast pace, meaning: Momma and daddy come home at the same time. They both have a check, benefits, 401Ks, retirement accounts and money in the bank. Momma is looking at daddy and daddy is looking at the home. Each one is asking, "What are you going to do?" We are definitely living in a new era where things are not the same anymore. So, if you try to have the same type of relationship with your spouse that your parents had, you will be faced with frustration because it doesn't work anymore. This is a new day. It's a 21st century day. I'm trying to shake us a little because it's time to wake up. This is the day and time we are living in now.

THE NEEDS OF A WOMAN

I believe our challenge as men, is to answer the age old, million dollar question (once again, I struggled with this myself and I know most of you have as well) which is: What does a woman want? What does she want from a real man? I believe women want equal submission. They are looking for us to respect them the same way we want to be respected. If we follow the principle of treating others the way we want to be treated, then we shouldn't have too many problems in the submission area. Don't expect anything from your wife that you won't expect from yourself. In other words, if you aren't "giving it," don't be expecting to receive it. It's not a one-sided relationship.Women are looking for shared responsibilities and duties because they are investing just as much into the relationship as we are. My wife once told me, "I want you to come home and invest just as much into the duties of this house as I do." She was looking for equal submission. When we realize we have our own unique gifts, it makes it easier to submit to one another.

The 21st century woman will yield to the governance and authority of her man. She will defer and consent, but let me give you the key: *you must be a man that's taking care of business!* If you're not taking care of business, I can guarantee you that you will face many challenges in your household. The 21st century woman is *not* the 19th or 20th century woman. She is a woman who understands she has been liberated through the Word of God. She also understands she has been liberated through our society and has been given the opportunity to use her gifts and skills which enable her to bring something to the table of life. I want to explore three things I believe the 21st century woman needs from a real man. Although she may never fully express these needs to you, they are some of a woman's deepest desires.

HER INTELLECTUAL NEEDS

The 21st century woman has a deeper understanding of the theological context of the Scripture than most pastors have. They have begun to understand what God is saying in His Word, and they are beginning to espouse their belief, value, and worth. They have adapted a new attitude which says, "You must understand where I am coming from or I don't need you anymore." I believe the message the 21st century woman is speaking to us as men today is: "We have no problems submitting to your authority, *if* you are willing to meet our intellectual, emotional, and spiritual needs." If you are willing to meet these three needs, there should be no submission problems in your relationship.

The first need I am sharing with you may not sound elaborate, but it is one of the most essential needs in a woman's life—communication. I promise you, this is one sure way to meet her intellectual needs. Women desire men who will engage in stimulating conversation and have positive input into the chaos of this life. If you are married, a basic need of a wife is to have intimate conversation with her husband. Let me clear something up for you, *intimate conversation* does not mean *sexual relations.* Sometimes as men we have a difficult time separating the two. We think just because we talk we have to go to the next level. Sometimes your spouse just wants to talk and go to sleep. If the truth be told, she really isn't too worried about the sexual relations as much as you. The reality is, most women can take the physical aspect of intimacy or leave it. If you haven't met her other needs then you shouldn't expect to have sexual relations with your wife. She isn't "feeling it" and will put the brakes on. She doesn't care how much you sweet talk her. If you haven't met her need for intimate conversation, you will be greeted with an attitude that says, "Listen, you can't even talk on my level or meet me where I need to be met. And now you think we're making love? I don't think so!" I'm trying to help you. I am a man speaking from experience.

We must purpose to communicate with the women in our lives. Most times, *men won't talk, and women never stop.* This is not a blanket statement. It's reality—it happens all the time. I believe sometimes our women think we don't speak English because when they are talking, we just sit there with a blank look on our face. They want a man who possesses substance and is willing to express it. They want men who can talk and appreciate something deeper than NFL and NBA. Women want men who will take the time to listen as they share about the complexities of their jobs or the intricacies of what's going on in their lives. When you stop and at least act like you are paying attention to what she is saying you are meeting her intellectual need. But we don't want to just pretend to listen; we want to strive to hear the heart of our women.

My wife serves on the Board of Directors for a financial institution. When she returned home from a three day meeting, she came home ready to share. She shared about the new responsibilities she had been assigned. She shared about the newly elected CEO, the new implementations and all types of new processes. She rattled down a list of several other things while I was sitting there blown away. Although, I was thinking, "Whoa! Sounds good to me," she didn't want me to just sit there and give no response or feedback. She didn't want me to say, "Yeah, baby, Dallas is playing tomorrow!" She wanted me to speak to her about what she had just shared on an intellectual level.

Most times, when we are unresponsive to our women, an invisible barrier is formed. It is one where you see each other, but you won't talk to each other. If you have developed a pattern of being unresponsive, communication will cease and your relationship will drift further and further apart. You will be like strangers living in the same house. It's true, sometimes as men, we just don't want to talk! And this is an area we have to continually work on. However, don't allow a wall to come between you and your wife. We must be aware of the strategic attack, especially to Christian men, to hinder the process of communication. If you have division between you, you will never meet your spouse's needs. The enemy desires to build a wall of partition between you and your spouse where you can't and won't communicate. He will make her feel she can't share the details of what is happening in her life. It's very important for you to talk to your wife. Recognize that when you don't talk to your wife, you are inviting separation into your relationship. When you allow separation to come, the enemy will take advantage of it. The result will be many undesirable things happening in your relationship. It will leave you scratching your head and wondering, "When did we grow apart instead of growing together?" Don't allow this to happen. Respond lovingly and thoughtfully to your wife.

You may ask, "What happens when we do get into intimate conversation, what are we going to say?" In most men's minds, we truly feel we don't have a lot to say. We are content going to work, bringing our paycheck home, paying the bills, eating our dinner and watching TV with remote in hand. Most men just want to relax when they come home. Women want to talk and ask questions. As men, we have to remember women are wired differently and think differently. We have to be sensitive, responsive, and compassionate to any concerns we feel are a waste of time to talk about. Most wives have fears and emotions they want to express but don't feel comfortable expressing them to their husbands. They want to ask questions. They want you to respond. They don't want a quick response, but a thoughtful one.

Women like to know what is going on. They like the inside scoop but despise getting "the run around." They want to know what is going on inside of your head, the household, etc. They want to ask questions like, "Are you still going to love me when I get old?" They know when you married them they were young and beautiful. We also know time brings about a change. Therefore, you have to continually communicate and reassure her of your love for her. When you reassure her, you are calming fears she may have and offering her a sense of security. Our role as men is to minister into the lives of our wives, so when there are questions on an issue, by all means reassure her.

Women want to be shown *how* the way is going to be made. Don't just tell them, "The Lord is going to make a way somehow." They want to know *how. How* is a way going to be made? Then they want to be shown how it's going to happen. Brothers, I have discovered two areas we don't like to deal with: sex and money. We will get spiritual when our wives are demanding an answer. We can even find supporting Scripture to back us up. But, this is the time to be honest with your wife. She will respect you and will have no problems submitting to you. So, make sure you make time for intimate conversation. It may start off with only a few moments, but at least get started. It takes time! You can't expect to just get into a long conversation and let that be the end of it! It shouldn't be every six months either. It should be an ongoing process where you develop a level of comfort, communion, and communication with one another. Gentlemen, you will reap a beautiful harvest in your relationship if you sow into her intellectual needs.

HER EMOTIONAL NEEDS

The second need a woman longs for from her man is to have her emotional needs met. A woman needs a man who can help keep her grounded. She needs a man who is willing to express himself and make it known that he cares about her. She is looking for lip service accompanied by actions. A man who will let his woman know I am concerned about you is meeting an emotional need. It really isn't hard to meet the emotional needs of a woman; it just takes a little consideration. For instance, if your wife's car is close to empty and you fill it up without her asking, you just met an emotional need. Even though she may not tell you, believe me, you just met a need in her life. What you just said to her was: I care! You just let her know she was so valuable to you that you didn't want her taking any chances with her life by running out of gas. Your actions told her you wanted to make sure she was covered and protected.

Your wife also needs to know she is meeting needs in your life that no other woman can meet. Knowing she is top priority in your life fulfills her emotional needs. I know we have female business partners, secretaries, co-workers, employees, ministry leaders and so on and all of these are important relationships which have some significant value to them. However, none of these relationships should ever take precedence over your wife. A wise man will realize he has to reassure his wife that she is unique and special and has a place in his life no one else can ever secure. Brothers, when your wife knows this, it releases you to another dimension in your marriage.

My wife knows there is a place in my life that no one else can fill, *but her*. I demonstrate this to her by giving her priority in my life. When I do this, it automatically lets her know she is unique and special to me. If she calls me, I'm there at a moment's notice for her. I've cancelled appointments for her that I probably won't cancel for anyone else. I love my church, I love my ministry and I love what God is doing, but if my wife needs me, I'm there for her. Why? She needs to know she holds a special place in my life.

In order for our wives to be top priority in our lives we have to recognize their value and worth. Your perception of your wife is very important. My wife is more than a wife; she is my helpmeet. Genesis 2:18 says, *"It is not good that man should be alone...I will make him a helpmeet."* God made somebody who will help meet the needs in a man's life. The word helpmeet does not mean doormat. It does not mean punching bag nor does it mean I can treat her any kind of way. God made my gift (my wife) and gave her to me. She is a virtuous woman and is more valuable than rubies (Proverbs 31:10). We must "wake up and smell the coffee." You have a blessing and a gift who can help you in everything you do; you just have to recognize her value. If I appreciate the gift God has given me, she can help meet the needs in my life. This means I have to identify the gifts in my wife's life and appreciate them. Some men don't understand the Word of God and look at their women as maids or baby producers. The word *helpmeet* means she is adaptable, suitable, and complimentary to your life. This is just what my wife is to me plus more. She is my best friend and confidant. Everything I do, I depend on her input into the situation. To be honest, it took me a long time to learn this. It took me a while to learn to get input from her *before* rather than *after*. So, it's important to find out her gifts in life. As I find out her gifts in life then I am able to help her to fulfill her purpose in life. When I help her to fulfill her purpose in life, the result is an emotionally satisfied woman.

Your wife must see you are making investments in her life that will fulfill her. Investing quality time in your relationship meets the emotional needs of a woman. Women love well-spent, uninterrupted time with their men. They live and long for it and when you do, you are ministering directly to their emotions. Once again, you are letting them know, "No one else is as endearing to me as you." My wife and I have a good time at home by ourselves. We are the same wherever we go. We don't put on a facade for our congregation or anyone else. We always have a good time because she holds a special place in my life. *No one* can fill the need in my life that she fills. So, I invest time in her privately.

Your wife's emotional needs are met when she doesn't have to worry about finances. Make sure provision is always made and from time to time financially bless your wife unexpectedly. Many times we have a hidden agenda, meaning: We tell our wives we are doing something for them, but in all actuality, it is really for ourselves. If you say you are working overtime for her, then do it! Don't say you are buying the sports car for her and she has to continue driving the beat up ride while you are driving the "promised" car. Don't tell her you are going to buy her a computer and then she can never use it because you are on it twenty-four/seven. Buy it for her and then allow her to drive it or use it in peace. We have to allow them to see we are making financial investments in their lives that will fulfill them.

Some additional examples of meeting your woman's emotional needs are when everyone else in the household is in the bed and you get up and check all the doors. You are conveying a message of concern for her well-being by securing the house. You are definitely talking her language. You are telling her you are going to keep her safe and not let anything happen to her. Gentlemen, that's like hitting a home run in a baseball game or scoring the winning points in a basketball game. Women need men who are willing to meet the emotional needs in their life by stepping up to the plate to protect and look out for their best interests.

Another way to meet a woman's emotional needs is to actually get things done without having to be asked. I will give you some more prime examples: the picture which has been leaning up against the wall for six months and you know she wants you to hang it on the wall; the unopened box lying on the floor waiting to be assembled; or the curtains laying across the sofa. Even though she hasn't asked you, you already know those things aren't there by happenstance. Gentlemen, if I come home and see some curtains or something draped across the sofa or the chair I sit in, I know they aren't laying there by mistake. If I see them laying there, I know what time it is. She wants me to put them up. It's the little things that meet needs in the lives of our women.

HER SPIRITUAL NEEDS

Third, but not least, a woman needs a man who can meet her spiritual needs. This means women desire and expect their men to have a personal thriving relationship with God. They are looking for their men to serve God for themselves and not to appease or to please them. They want a man who is deep enough in God not to bring discord or stress into the relationship. You can't accomplish this if you don't have a personal relationship with God. Stress or discord will always be present without God.

A man who has a personal relationship with God recognizes he has to be deep enough to meet her spiritual needs and meeting her spiritual needs means establishing his own relationship with God. There has to be an attitude which says, "I'm going to serve God no matter what my wife does, no matter what my wife says, or no matter what life brings my way."

Men, we must make our declaration and stand by it: "I'm going to have my *own* personal relationship with God!" Brothers, this is the only way you can truly minister to your wife by being in relationship with God. You will need to hear from Him. Just in case you forgot, women's minds think very fast (I know my wife does). In this area alone you must be able to receive discernment and revelation from God in order to effectively minister to the spiritual needs in your wife's life. I am a living witness, it can only be done by developing a strong relationship with God for yourself.

Most importantly, never forget your wife is a mirror image of your spiritual condition. Never forget you carry the seed of life. Whatever seed you plant into her, she is going to give back one hundred fold. If you plant bitterness into her, and she is bitter towards you, where does she get it from? YOU! We are the givers of life, she is the incubator of life. So whatever you plant, it's going to grow you a harvest. Most times women will give more back to you than you give. If you give her a little bit of love, she'll give you a whole lot of love back. If you give her a little bit of bitterness, she'll give you a whole lot of bitterness back. If you give her one smart word, she'll give you a whole lot of smart words back and cut you up!

When things start getting chaotic, hectic, and out of sync in my home, I have to check "me" out. I have to stop and say, "What is going on?" The husband as the head must stop and see what's wrong and repair the damage.

Genesis 3:16 reveals that a woman's desire is toward her man. She wants to please you. She wants to be a helpmeet to you. But, you must be in a relationship with God where we are receiving nurture, instruction, and direction. When you are, He gives you the prescription needed to minister to your woman's spiritual needs. You are able to speak into her life and give positive affirmations. You will know how to plant seeds in those areas where you want to see growth in her life. *She is a mirror of your spiritual relationship with the Lord.* Remember, you cannot meet her spiritual needs if yours haven't been met.

WHAT A REAL WOMAN WANTS

One of the ministers in my congregation sent me an e-mail that I felt was very appropriate to share. I shared it at our Women's Conference because it was so in tune with the message I was going to be preaching at the time. The minister who sent me the e-mail had no clue of the topic I was going to minister, so, it became one of those, 'WOW God, this is right where I am!' moments. I believe I would be remiss if I didn't share this e-mail with you as well. It is entitled, *What Does a Real Woman Want?*

> In a brief conversation a man asked a woman he was pursuing the question, "What kind of man are you looking for?" She sat quietly for a moment before looking him in the eye and asking, "Do you really want to know?" Reluctantly, he said, "yes." She began to expound: "As a woman in this day and age, I am in a position to ask a man what he can do for me that I can't do for myself? I pay my own bills. I take care of my household without the help of any man or woman for that matter. I am in a position to ask, 'What can you bring to the table?' The man looked at her and clearly thought she was referring to money. She quickly corrected his thought and stated, "And I'm not referring to money. I need more. I need a man who is striving for perfection in every aspect of his life."

> He sat back in his chair, folded his arms and asked her to explain. She said, "I'm looking for someone who is striving for perfection mentally because I need conversation and mental stimulation. I don't need a simple minded man. I'm looking for someone who is striving for perfection spiritually. I don't need to be unequally yoked. Believers mixed with unbelievers is a recipe for disaster. And even if he is a believer he needs to believe as I do. I need a man who is striving for excellence financially because I don't need a financial burden. I'm looking for

someone who is sensitive enough to keep me grounded when I go through changes. I don't need a man who is going to purposely bring me grief. I'm looking for someone I can respect in order to be submissive. I must respect him and he must respect me. I cannot be submissive to a man who isn't taking care of his business or who is messy in his personal affairs. I have no problem being submissive but he has to be worthy. God made woman to be a helpmate for man. I can't help a man if he can't help himself. If he can't help himself then he definitely can't help me."

When she finished her spill she looked at him. He sat there with a puzzled look on his face and he said, "You're asking for a lot." And she replied, "I am worth a lot!"

I have simply been trying to challenge us to think. I want us to think beyond the old paradigms and nuisances. We must think beyond the way it used to be. We must deal with the reality of life as we know it today. Whether you are married or single, what we have discussed in this chapter are realities. They stretch us, challenge us, pull us, and tug at us. The operative conclusion of this matter is simply what Paul said in Ephesians 5:21—we must submit ourselves one to another as unto the Lord.

As a man and as the head, we are to love our women as Christ loved the church. Remember, we answered the question, "How did He love the church?" Christ gave Himself expecting nothing in return. This is the same reason we serve Him today because He paid the price. My dear brother, you have a responsibility to love your wife without strings being attached just as Christ loved us. Women have to know that you love them in spite of.

There is a price we must pay. It won't be paid on daddy's ticket or on what we thought it meant to be a man. It will be paid when we align ourselves with the correct Scriptural context, develop and maintain a personal relationship with God, and begin to lead our families into the desired places God has for us. It's paid by submitting ourselves one to another in the Lord. The passage of Scripture in Ephesians simply revealed, just as Christ did some difficult things for the church, we too, must be willing to do some for our wives. We must be willing to give it all up for her, just as Christ did for us. We are commanded to love our wives as Christ loved the church.

The church did nothing for Jesus as long as He was alive. It wasn't until He died that they began to want to perfume His body and take care of Him. Men, it is not until we die to our male dominance and to our superiority in ourselves that we will begin to get the perfume like Christ did.

STAND YOUR GROUND

Sisters, if you're not married yet, watch out for a man who only comes to church because he's with you. Don't be afraid to inquire about the length of time the gentleman has been going to church before he met you. You also want to know if he is going to be committed to the Lord and stay in church. You must understand, men will use church to manipulate you. If you're not careful you will become involved with a spiritually inferior man who can cause you to stunt your growth in the Lord. He may try to take you from where you are in the Lord and put you into some place that is below his level. He does this because of his own esteem issues, insecurities and inferiority complex that haven't been dealt with. If he hasn't committed himself to developing a ip with God, he definitely doesn't want you to have relationship with God. For that reason, he's intimidated by the relationship, and it challenges the very existence of his manhood. Stand your ground!

CHAPTER FOUR

Man Wanted: Dead or Alive?

Most times when we hear about a wanted man, our minds may immediately think of *America's Most Wanted* television show or the FBI's Most Wanted List. We automatically think of men who are wanted fugitives. When I am referring to *Man Wanted*, I am referring to *you!* You are a *wanted man* whether you know it or not. You are a wanted man in the Kingdom of God, in your family and in our society. You are wanted to be a better man, husband, father, brother, uncle, and friend in this 21st century.

In order for God to perform His will and get you to your destination in life, you must completely surrender yourself to Him. You must turn yourself over to God and allow Him to take you to a place where you deal with your private issues, such as: machoism, male dominance, selfishness, not accepting responsibility, dependency on others and so on. The place God will take you is not easy, yet it is rewarding. Yes, we are wanted men, but our real challenge and question is: dead or alive? As you read on you will begin to understand this question more and more. Let's take a look at the life of a well known man named David. I believe there are many lessons we can learn from his life.

> *David therefore departed thence, and*
> *escaped to the cave Adullam: and when his*

*brethren and all his father's house heard it,
they went down thither to him. And every one
that was in distress, and every one that was
in debt, and every one that was discontented,
gathered themselves unto him; and he
became a captain over them: and there were
with him about four hundred men. And David
went thence to Mizpeh of Moab: and he said
unto the king of Moab, Let my father and my
mother, I pray thee, come forth, and be with
you, till I know what God will do for me. And
he brought them before the king of Moab: and
they dwelt with him all the while that David
was in the hold. And the prophet Gad said
unto David, Abide not in the hold; depart, and
get thee into the land of Judah. Then David
departed, and came into the forest of Hareth.*

—1 Samuel 22:1-5

I want to look at how the life of David parallels with the life of a man who is seeking to fulfill his purpose and destiny. In the above passage of scripture, David had a death warrant out on his life. King Saul had enlisted and employed hit men to literally take David out. In fleeing for his life, David found himself in the cave of Adullam. He went into the cave to hide, seek solitude, and find safety to preserve his life. He didn't understand that not only was he on Saul's hit man's list, He was also on God's. Saul wanted him physically dead. God *needed* him to die in another way, in order to fulfill his destiny in life. The cave became the place where David died and was resurrected as a new man.

MAN GOING INTO THE CAVE

"David therefore departed thence, and escaped to the cave Adullam" (1 Samuel 22:1). The cave in its initial stages is

representative of a tomb. It represents David entering into a place where he had to deal with his issues. When David entered into the cave, it brought him to a place of contemplation which caused him to mull over his life. He had to think about *how?* "How could I have been on the mountaintop yesterday, and today I'm buried inside a tomb?" He was no longer a loved and admired man. He had become a hated, despised, and rejected man. He had become a man who was being bitterly ridiculed and chased like a common criminal. He was a man who had no other place to retreat, but to the cave. I can envision David wondering in his mind, "What happened? I was just being hailed and celebrated by all of Israel. *I was it!*" David had just won a tremendous victory over Goliath, been esteemed as the greatest warrior who ever lived, and had been awarded the king's daughter. It was this same David who in the midst of all of his glory was now—a wanted man!

As a man, can you imagine being on the mountaintop one day and the next you are despised and rejected? Some men may look at their household and wonder the same thing, "What happened? I used to be the apple of my wife's eye. My children who once loved me want nothing to do with me. What happened to me? What is going on in my life?" You are facing Adullam when everything that once boosted or lifted you up isn't there anymore!

Every man faces an Adullam in his life. It doesn't matter whether you have identified yourself as a metro, retro, patriarch, power seeker or even a *real man*. You will at one time or another face Adullam. Adullam is a place of rejection. Adullam for all intents and purposes was a place of David's death. God had to take David into this cave of Adullam so that he would become introspective. David described his anguish and his loneliness in the cave when he said, *"I looked on my right hand, and beheld, but there was no man that would know me: refuge failed me; no man cared for my soul"* (Psalms 142:4). I want you to understand that it's in the failures, rejections, betrayals, faults, and the mess ups of our lives that we enter our cave or tomb. You can call it your cave or your tomb, but one thing is for sure, it becomes our place of Adullam which is a place of reflection and learning. When desperation drives us to our cave of reflection and learning, something happens to us. We actually come to grips with who we are, what we are and what our purpose is. It is a place where we can get ourselves together by reflecting on all the things that have transpired in our lives. I believe it is a place God calls us to in order for us to die to ourselves. (Don't close the book now, we are just getting started.) We all know death is not an easy thing. Death is not a welcomed thing. Death is not something we look forward to, but in order to live, David had to die. We must do likewise. Once again, every man faces an Adullam.

WHAT HAPPENED IN THE CAVE?

Since we now know we will have a cave experience at one time or another in our lives and know God will call us to this place, let's explore this issue a little further. You may be wondering, what happened while David was in the cave of Adullam? What transpired while David was isolated from everyone? First, David came to the realization that he needed God. It wasn't a deep revelation. He looked at his situation and his circumstances and realized it wasn't his father, mother, or brothers, but he who needed God. Even in the midst of being surrounded by enemies, he knew it was he who needed God. Second, he realized he had to die to himself. He learned what it meant to be a man who had to confront his issues. David's isolation from everyone forced him to reconcile and deal with himself. I'm sure at one point or another he felt he was in this predicament because of Saul, his brothers, or the prophet, Samuel. I am sure David had a whole list of reasons as to why he was in the cave, but then ultimately came to the conclusion: I am in the cave because I need to deal with me! David knew he had to deal with himself in the cave in order for God to get him where He wanted him to be.

A PLACE OF SOLITUDE

There is a place where all we've done won't work anymore and we are forced into a place of solitude. It is essential for every man to visit this place. David faced his ultimate foe in the place of solitude. It is there you will also face yours. The ultimate foe every man will have to face one day is: *HIMSELF!* Most of us don't want to look at ourselves because it's easier to look at someone else. It's easier when our mentality is: "It's your fault...," or "If you hadn't..." or "If you would just...then I would be..." Many times we think it is everyone else blocking and keeping us from making progress in life. We think it's our family, our spouse, our children, our friends, our boss, or others holding us back.

Many have the David mentality where we would rather blame things on someone else rather than accept responsibility. For instance, sometimes as a pastor, I can be blamed for everything that goes wrong in a person's life. The mentality of some is:

> "Life would be better if Bishop would only have more altar calls, or if Bishop would let the choir sing more, or if Bishop would just let me prophesy or if Bishop would let me do this or do that...then the church would run smoother and we would be happier."

But, it's not just me who takes the blow; sometimes these same people blame their wives, their children, their supervisors, etc. They hit them with the blame mentality.

Have you ever stopped to think you are in your own way? We must understand the concept that we need to get ourselves out of the way and we need God's help to do it. David had to come to the point where he realized he didn't know it all! Most men, today, are where David was—in their own little cave thinking they know it all, can do it all and have the answer to all. As men, we sometimes believe if everyone does it our way, everything will be okay. I believe God dealt with David about "not having it going on." I believe God showed him the real challenge was not *who* was messing with him or *who* was in his way—it was for David—to get out of his own way. We can be the biggest hindrance in our lives. However, the solitude of the cave is exclusively designed to help us lose the mentality of others being the problem. The cave helps us to discern that we have been the ultimate enemy hindering our own progress and dreams in life. What God has assigned for you to do, no person or thing can stop it—*except you!* Instead of running from solitude, we must make the same choice as David. We must disconnect from our flesh and reconnect with God in the solitude of the cave.

There is one important principle I think we should remember about David. He developed an intimate relationship with God while tending sheep. I believe David lost his intimacy with God when he was elevated from the back side of the mountain to the platform with the status of being *somebody*. I suppose when David felt he had become *somebody*, he began to think he could utilize his own strength and abilities to achieve his accomplishments. Even so, God has an awesome way of bringing us back to our knees and letting us know without Him, we are nothing. Solitude is a place

God will lead us to in order to remind us of this fact.

A PLACE OF VENTING

"I cry to the Lord with my voice; with my voice to the Lord do I make supplication. I pour out my complaint before Him; I tell before Him my trouble. When my spirit was overwhelmed and fainted [throwing all its weight] upon me, then You knew my path. In the way where I walk they have hidden a snare for me." (Psalm 142:1-3 AMP). David found himself in an unsettling emotional state. He probably felt like no one wanted to help him, no one cared, no one wanted to be on his side and no one had his back. In this passage of Scripture, David was expressing his heartfelt feelings to God. It seems David learned he could vent to the Lord. He learned Adullum wasn't a place to be macho and hold your true feelings in. Instead, it was the place to let it all out. He let God know how overwhelmed and burdened he was by all the weight he felt he had to carry. He even put his finger in the face of God and said, *"...You knew my path. In the way where I walk they have hidden a snare for me."* It was almost like David said, "God, you know what they did to me and what I'm going through. You see where I am! Why don't you get my brothers, Saul, and the ones trying to kill me? God, why are you allowing me to go through all of this?"

I'm sure David was used to God intervening on his behalf. They had a history of working together. When the bear attacked him; he was able to kill the bear. When the lion threatened the flock; he was able to kill the lion. When he had to face the giant Goliath; he was able to kill him. In spite of his many victories, David found himself at a point where everything he touched appeared to be messed up. He must have wondered where God was and why He didn't intervene like He used to. Fair enough to say, David was angry with

God. He said, *"Look on the right hand [the point of attack] and see; for there is no man who knows me [to appear for me]. Refuge has failed me and I have no way to flee; no man cares for my life or my welfare"* (Psalm 142:4 AMP).

Have you been in situations where you wonder why God didn't intervene to help you out? Have you ever felt God was unfair at times? I know I have. I've been in situations where I've said, "God, You know what I'm going through...where are You?"

Have you ever just vented to God telling Him what is truly and honestly on your heart? (Women probably have this down pat, but this is something men must continually work on.) Do you ever remember a time in your life when you just needed to ask God why? "Why are You allowing me to go through all of this hell? Why all of the trials and tribulations? Why all the pain? Why all the disappointments and failures? Why, God, why?"

Maybe you have never been in a destitute situation like David was. Maybe you've never felt like everything and everybody was against you. Maybe you've never felt like God doesn't know what's going on. God knew David all too well—Just as He knows you and me! God knew about David's dismay, heartache, pain, frustrations, and turmoil. God knew everything that was going on in David's life. Yet, He still allowed David to experience the pain of human life and also allowed him an opportunity to vent to Him about it. I questioned God as I studied these scriptures because God was fully aware of all the hardships in David's life. He knew this man was alone and alienated. God knew everything precious to him had been taken away. Therefore, my question was, "God, why did you allow him to go through all of those trials?" I believe it was because God wanted to show David a better way to live.

A PLACE OF REFUGE

In addition to the cave being a place of solitude and a place to vent to God, it was a place of refuge. Not only was it a safe haven, it was a perfect environment for God to teach David some valuable lessons. He taught David to die to his selfishness, dependency on others, and to the allure of self preservation. God taught him to die to his passions, his desires, his wants, and his will. I'm sure David's process to die to himself wasn't easy. I can imagine the struggle between him and his flesh, dealing with thoughts like, "I thought the king was going to do right by me...he wants to kill me...my brothers rejected me..." All the while, I'm sure God was saying, 'David, die to those things...give them up...I'm your Source!" When David went into the cave he wasn't the great giant slayer, he wasn't the mighty man of valor, he wasn't David who had the favor of God. He was just David. In the cave it was just David and God. It was the Teacher and His student.

David said, *"I cried to You, O Lord; I said, You are my refuge, my portion in the land of the living"* (Psalm 142:5). As a result, the cave that once buried him became a shelter from the worries of the world. It became a sanctuary where he could disconnect from others and reconnect with God. God taught David that the cave was not a place of sulking, but a place of significance. In the cave David could see what God was doing in his mundane life. Being alone with God gave Him an opportunity to speak to David about his life. After God speaks, what else is there to say? David had learned to put an end to all of his whining, complaining and mourning. He finally realized the most blessed thing was being connected to God.

We too, can go to this place where we can refocus on our mundane life and reconnect with God. When I go to this place, I am not Bishop, I am not Daddy, I am not husband, I am not Mr. Know It All. It is little "me" with my "Big God." I know I'm no good to anyone until I go to my safe haven and connect with God. When we grasp the cave experience, a miraculous thing begins to occur—*life!*

THE FRUIT OF THE CAVE: DEATH UNTO LIFE

Look at what transpired in David's life after being in the cave, contemplating and seeking God's face. He was given this revelation, *"Bring my life out of prison, that I may confess, praise, and give thanks to Your name; the righteous will surround me and crown themselves because of me, for You will deal bountifully with me"* (Psalm 142:7). David went into the cave complaining, whining, mourning, and sulking, but as you see, his whole attitude changed. It was no longer about David being promoted, liked or appreciated anymore. It was about living a lifestyle of praise and thanksgiving. It was *all* about being in a right relationship with God.

The fruit produced from the cave was praise, thanksgiving, humility, and dependency on God. David went in as a *dead man* but later came out alive. Although David died in the prison of the cave, it became a place of birth for a new outlook. I truly believe once we give birth to a new outlook for our lives and understand it's not what we can get out of others, our lives will change. I really believe David's attitude was much like ours can be at times: *'I'm David, don't you see and know who I am? I was anointed by Samuel. I am somebody!'* The cave was the place where God had to crush David and his attitude. It's when you are naked and all alone you find you really aren't all of that! David learned in spite of all of his many abilities that he could not control people.

I believe it's important to understand this. If you don't, you will always be looking for what others can do for you. You will always look for others to help you promote your agenda. David learned in his cave experience that promotion and God's favor doesn't come from others. It comes from having a true connection with God.

When David came out of the cave he stopped being dependent on the applause of people. Rather than listening for the cheers of others, he listened to the voice of God. When there is nobody to sing your praises—it's a humbling thing. When you are in no man's land and nobody knows you—it's a humbling thing. When nobody even cares that you are somebody—it's a humbling thing. When God let's you know that your title, your position, your job, or your popularity doesn't mean anything to Him—it's a humbling thing. Humility is the fruit produced in our lives when we are broken and laying prostrate before God.

David was noted in the Scriptures for being a man after the heart of God. Even though David had a whole lot of flaws and faults in his life; he still was a man after the heart of God. He loved God and learned that everything he would accomplish in life would come from his relationship with God. He discovered he could repent of his faults and major mess-ups and still love and worship God. Even though we have faults and major mess-ups, we too, can still love and worship God. We still have to get into a position where we can praise God, no matter what! When we die to self and stop being dependent on the masses and realize God is our Source, God can do something in our lives.

In this 21st century, if we plan on doing anything great for God, we've got to be men after the heart of God. We've got to be men who are passionate about the things of God.

We've got to be men who love God more than life itself. We've got to be men who stay in God's presence long enough to receive answers to the complexities of life, get wisdom and strength for the day and receive our provision from His hands for our lives. Apostle Paul shares a secret of how we can become men after God's heart today: *"[I assure you] by the pride which I have in you in [your fellowship and union with] Christ Jesus our Lord, that I die daily [I face death every day and die to self]"* (1 Corinthians 15:31 AMP). We've got to die everyday. Everyday we've got to have a cave experience. Everyday we've got to get into a place where we disconnect from others. As long as you are dependent on others, then your flesh, your well-being, and your "ism" are defined by people and not by God. God wants us at the place where we've seen David and Paul who both learned God wanted to be the only one to define them. We too, must come to that point in our lives where we are willing to die daily and allow God to define us.

I've learned I have to die daily to *me* because *me* wants the popularity, *me* wants to be liked, *me* wants to be appreciated, *me* wants to be stroked, *me* wants to be in the limelight, *me* wants to be lifted up. But I've learned that I have to die to *me*. I've got to die to that which causes *me* to become what others think I should be. I've got to die so my dependency is not on *me* or you, but my dependency is on God.

THE SECRET OF THE CAVE

If you don't remember anything else you have read, please remember this: Connecting and being in tune with God releases a dynamic in your spiritual life which produces favor that attracts others to you. The law of attraction was one of the main results from time well spent with God. David discovered the secret of the cave, although, it didn't remain a secret when he came out because others noticed and were attracted to him. While David went into the cave with a death warrant on his head, being despised, rejected, and alienated, he came out a *wanted man.* No longer was he wanted dead. He was now wanted *ALIVE!*

"And every one that was in distress, and every one that was in debt, and every one that was discontented, gathered themselves unto him; and he became a captain over them: and there were with him about four hundred men" (1 Samuel 22:2). David's cave experience put him into a leadership position where he became a captain over four hundred men. The very people David wanted to be on his side were now drawn to him. He didn't have to force, deceive, manipulate, impress, or try to win anyone. He didn't even have to go out and solicit people saying, "Vote for me...I'm your man!...I'm out of the cave now...I'm getting ready to...come over here and join me." No, David didn't attempt to buy, cater, or persuade any man. The Bible says, *"every one that was in distress and in debt, and every one that was discontented, gathered themselves unto him."* It seems they just started coming from the north, south, east, and west. I believe David even attracted individuals who at one point despised him. Why? They saw the anointing of God on his life and were drawn to him. God just had to get David into the cave so He could speak to him.

When you get in the presence of God and seek Him with all of your heart, soul, and mind, He will begin to give you the very desires of your heart. You won't have to promote yourself either. You won't have to go on television and make commercials. You won't have to tell others how great and anointed you are. You won't have to tell people about how God has blessed you. God will cause you to become a light. Just like moths are drawn to a light, so will others be drawn to you. Remember, it won't be any of your boastful skills; it will be the anointing on your life.

This passage of Scripture has strong implication for marriages, families, church growth, and even for social relationships. The lesson implies that hurting people are drawn to believers who are connected to God. Husband, your wife will be drawn to you, *if* she sees you are connected to God. Your children, co-workers and friends will all be drawn when they see the connection. If you are a pastor, people will be attracted to your ministry, *if* they see you are connected to God.

I shared with my congregation at one point that we don't have to have mega television commercials. We don't have to put billboards up. We don't have to try to advertise who we are as Calvary Community Church. If our church is full of members who are connected to God then people who are hurting will be drawn to our ministry. It's not about how well I preach, or how well the choir sings or how great the musicians are. It's about how connected we are to God! When we're connected to God, hurting people will automatically be drawn to us. They will seek after the anointing that's on our lives. Do you wonder why divorcees, AIDS victims or the poor are drawn to you? They see the anointing and presence of God on your life. That's what makes a church grow. It's not about more sophisticated programs; it's about people who are connected to God. When you are connected to God, the hurting are connected to you. It happens every time people sense *help* on your life. When David became a worshipper and got back into a right position with God, the people came. They came then and only then.

When was the last time a hurting person came to you? When is the last time someone said, "There is something different about you?" When was the last time someone asked for what you had and you were able to share Jesus with them? When you are connected to God, you don't have to sell your program, put it in the media, or beg folks to come to your event. People will just come simply because they sense the anointing of God on your life.

All God needs is one willing vessel who will seek His face and have a compassionate heart to those who are discontented, hurting, in debt, and longing. He wants to use you. After David's cave experience, I believe he said, "God, if you can use anybody then use me." God is looking for men in this 21st century who are willing to deal with hurting people. We have people who are longing and looking for hope today. God needs men and women who have been in His presence to intensify and give a spiritual answer to a spiritual problem. Many of the problems we are facing in our society today cannot be fixed by another pill or another therapy session. Some issues require having hands laid on, some need deliverance, while some need a Word from the Lord. It may require some men to turn down their plates and intercede on the behalf of others. People are longing for those who have been in the presence of God to discern the hurt, heartache and pain in their lives. They need someone who can speak life into their destitute situations. This 21st century needs men who will come out of the cave inspired from being in the presence of God. The cave is the source and strength of your inspiration. The cave is the thing that's going to draw them. We are the source of God's inspiration.

A PLACE OF RESTORATION

"...and when his brethren and all his father's house heard it, they went down thither to him" (1 Samuel 22:1b). A phenomenal thing happened in this passage of Scripture. Not only were the discontent and broken drawn to David, but his family was drawn back to him. The Bible says when

he came out of the cave his family started looking for him. It's something about a man being in his God-assigned place. When something is happening in your life, your family is the first to notice. When it really happens and you come out of the cave they will be drawn to the anointing on your life. You won't have to say a word about being in the presence of God. They will see a difference and will tell others about it. You won't have to get a billboard or a poster made with your name on it stating that you are a new person who is saved, sanctified, and full of the Holy Ghost now.

It's amazing to me, when David came out of the cave he was sought by the same brothers whose attitudes were, "who do you think you are?" The same family members who earlier rejected and ridiculed David came to the cave looking for him. God was restructuring David's family. The one who was a subject of disdain by his brothers is now being sought after to become the Messianic King who will bring order. His family finally recognized him as a leader and came to him. You may have been the outcast or the black sheep in your family, but when you get into a place of Adullam where you reconnect with God—things change!

THE POWERFUL LESSONS OF THE CAVE

There were three powerful lessons David learned in the cave of Adullam. Every man who believes God for the next level of increase should adhere to these three things David learned: He learned to stand alone and be misunderstood, to do more than is expected, and to operate in a spirit of excellence.

LEARN TO STAND ALONE AND BE MISUNDERSTOOD

If you're going to do great exploits for God, you can't do it by pleasing other people. Pleasing people and being driven by their opinions is something you will have to be completely delivered from. You've got to get this in your spirit right now. As we have previously discussed, David learned in the cave that he couldn't even depend on his own family. When he went to battle with Goliath and the Philistines, he was opposed by his own blood. His brothers turned their backs on him and questioned him, "Who do you think you are? Why do you think you're so good? Why aren't you at home tending the sheep?" Sometimes the ones closest to you won't always appreciate the value God has placed on your life. You must learn the valuable lesson that you may have to stand alone and be misunderstood before you are able to go where God desires to take you. For every person who is willing to accept the call of God and step into his assigned destiny, there will be a *hundred* people who don't understand *why* and *how* you do things the way you do. If those *hundred* people haven't been in the presence of God like you have and haven't received the same revelation you've received, then they won't see or hear what you do. They may see with carnal eyes and hear with fleshly ears. But, you will be able to use your spiritual eyes to see and your anointed ears to hear what God has called you to do because you've been in His presence. This allows you to be in the position that even if no one else jumps on board and showers you with support, you will accomplish what God assigned you to do. You have to remember, it's not their assignment; *it's your assignment.* God didn't call them to do that specific assignment—*He called you to do it.*

David came out of the cave of Adullam anointed by God. He wasn't looking to the left or to the right. He didn't solicit and politicize for a crowd to follow him. He just walked out of the cave in the anointing and power of God. He had become a man on a mission. A man on a mission is a *focused man.* A man that's anointed of God is a man who is fully acquainted with his assignment from God. He knows what has to be done and knows where he is going. He is a man who lives life on purpose. After spending time with God, David aligned his life with God's will for his life. He also came to the conclusion that if this meant he was misunderstood and no one caught his vision, he was still anointed by God and would perform the things assigned to him by God.

When you are able to say, "God, I'm willing to do whatever it takes to have your favor and anointing. I am willing to do whatever it takes in order to hear from You again," the anointing will come. The anointing is not what people think of your life. Most Christians today want to be anointed so others can see they are anointed. We strut our spiritual prowess by saying, "Oh, the Lord showed me a Scripture...God gave me a WORD...the Lord showed me this and told me to tell you...I'm praying for you, and because I'm praying you're going to be blessed." Listen, if you are anointed of God you don't have to strut your spiritual prowess in front of me or anyone else. All you have to do is walk humbly before your God. Whatever God has for you He will give to you. Whatever is supposed to happen for you, will happen, whether someone tells you about it or not.

There are many men who have been called by God to do great things but they are apprehensive because of the opinions of others. They are overly concerned about what people will say or how they will look at them if they attempt to step into what God has assigned for their life. If you are fearful of people then God may be calling you into the cave. You may not be as anointed as you thought you were. When you are anointed of God you don't care what people say. All you will care about is what God says. All you want to hear Him say is, *"Well done, my good and faithful servant!"* If no one ever places you on a platform, gives you any applause or celebrates you, all you should care about is pleasing God.

After all, you don't do what you do to gain and garner the applause of others. You do what you do because you love God and because you are anointed by God.

I understand this principle very well because I am a pastor. I do what I do because I love God and I am anointed by God. I do it whether someone claps, says "Amen, praise the Lord" or whether someone agrees with me or not. I hear what God is speaking to me and I articulate what I've heard from the Lord. I am very God-driven in the way I lead my congregation because it is not *my will* or *my way* but *God's will* that is to be done. Bishop Francisco died to self, and he's no longer alive. It is Christ Jesus who lives in me (Galatians 2:20).

I cannot say it enough: when God assigns you to a thing, you've got to be willing to stand alone and be misunderstood. When God calls you, other individuals will hate you, lie on you, mistreat you, talk about you, put you down, and they'll even ask you, "Who do you think you are?" One of the things we are challenged with in our society today is everybody is speaking to us. Everybody thinks they know what is best for us. They are trying to tell us what to do, when to do it and how to do it. While people are wanting to speak over our lives, there is One Whose name is Jehovah Who wants to speak more. He wants to commune and fellowship with us. God is looking and longing for us to come into a place where we can hear His voice clearly. He wants His sheep to know His voice so they will not follow a stranger. God is looking for men who aren't swayed by popular opinion. Family members will try to take you back into your past to remind you that they know who you are. They will give you the "I remember when..." and "You ain't nobody special!" speech. You've got to inform them that the little snotty nosed kid doesn't live there anymore. Let them know you are determined to complete your God-given assignment, whether they believe it or not. You must understand, when you stand up and

84

declare who you are and Whose you are, you don't have to garner support. People will seek after you, but just remember, it's not about you. It's about the Spirit of God dwelling on the inside of you. It's about the anointing of God on your life.

We've got to come to grips with the fact that, it's not about our physique, our money, our position, our automobiles, our looks, or what we possess. It is about the anointing of God. After all, it's the anointing of God your wife yearns for. It is the anointing of God that your children desire. It is the presence of God your family is craving. It's the anointing of God your supervisor wants. People are drawn to you because the anointing of God is present in your life. When you sense the anointing on your life then you will be able to stand alone and be misunderstood. When everyone else is going left, you will be able to say, "I hear the Spirit of the Lord say, go right." You may feel like you don't understand it or like you can't explain it. In fact, I can't put it into perspective or articulate all the *why's*, but you will know it is the way you are suppose to go.

There are times God tells me to do things I can't even explain to my wife. I don't understand all of the ins and outs myself. I don't understand *why* and it doesn't make a whole lot of sense to me, but something on the inside is telling me this is the way we need to go. Thank God for a supportive wife who also knows the ways of God. When these moments occur, she simply says, "If God says do it, then I've got to support you 110%! So, let's go for it!" You may not have this type of support or be able to explain to others the vision that God has given to you, but one thing remains: you must be willing to stand alone and be misunderstood to do the great exploits God has ordained for your life.

DO MORE THAN IS EXPECTED

The second thing I want you to recognize is this: If you're going to do great things for God, you've got to do more than what's expected of you. If you study the life of David you will discover his life had a lot of flaws and challenges, but he always did more than what was expected. As I stated before, the Bible declared David to be a man after the heart of God. He understood the throbbing heartbeat of God. Even when he fell into sin, David cried out to God and repented. He knew he had fallen short, sinned, and made a mess. However, he was always willing to do more than was required, even if it meant sacrifice. Others in the same situation may not even acknowledge their sin, but David did more than was required.

David realized he couldn't just do the mediocre things; he had to do more than what was expected of him. He acknowledged he was a leader who had been placed in the forefront. So therefore, he knew he must be first partaker. If we are going to do great things for God, we can't send other people to do our work. Sometimes when we are facing a tough situation we may send other people to take the hit for us, knowing we are the leader. We may round up others so that we won't be killed by criticism and unpopularity. A man who does more than is expected will always step up, assume responsibility, and do more than is required to put things back on the right track. You've got to do more than is expected of you in order to do what God called you to do.

OPERATE IN A SPIRIT OF EXCELLENCE

The third thing David learned was to operate with a spirit of excellence. God can't use us if we are not willing to operate with a spirit of excellence. We have to position ourselves and everything we do as "unto the Lord." This includes our jobs, our homes, our ministry and every arena of our life which must be done "unto the Lord." If you don't do something wholeheartedly "unto the Lord," there is no way it was done in a spirit of excellence. We have to continually say, "Father, everything I do, I do it as unto You."

Operating in a spirit of excellence causes us to be attracted to things of eternal value. All the monuments and the things we try to build will all fall and crumble. Only what's done for the kingdom of God will last. Only the lives you touch and impact for Christ are going to count. Only the ministries you invest in that are investing into the souls of others are going to make a difference. Once again, all of the monuments and all the things we build and aspire to as Christians today don't mean anything unless they have eternal value. I'm even going to put pastors out here. Aspiring to have a jet is nice; however, having a jet doesn't mean anything in Heaven. All of the "stuff" we acquire and boast about means nothing. It's only what we do for the kingdom of God that's going to make a difference and where excellence will prevail. When David was resurrected as a new man from the cave he realized his eternal destiny. When he understood the true value of what he was doing, excellence propelled in his life.

'NO PARKING' IN THE CAVE

After you've been in the cave for awhile, you do have to come out. I believe this is a challenge to many of us today. Once we get in the presence of God, we don't want to come out. We want to stay right there. We want to stay in a holy huddle for the rest of our lives. We want to stay in a place where we are anointed of God. We want to stay shut in with "me, myself and I." God has a different plan. After we've saturated in His presence, He desires for us to "go" so others can be drawn to us. There is a 'no parking' zone in the cave. If we park in the cave, we aren't any good to anyone, and a difference will never be made.

"Then the prophet Gad said to David, Do not remain in the stronghold; leave, and get into the land of Judah. So David left and went into the forest of Hareth" (1 Samuel 22:5). What the prophet was saying to David in a nice way was, "Get out!" God brought David into his place of destiny after he was resurrected as a new man. He brought him into a place where he could release him to fulfill his purpose. I want you to understand David wasn't mistake-free when he came out of the cave. The only way we're going to get what God has for us is to stay in relationship with Him. God doesn't care how bad we mess up; He just wants us to stay connected. He doesn't care how bad we think we are, just keep coming back to the cave. Remember, the cave is about you and your relationship with God and is the source and strength of your inspiration. God broke David down in the cave to show him that all his things, abilities, and skills meant nothing without God. But, He also built David up and let him know He was going to use him. David was ready and fully equipped to deal with the world when he departed from the cave.

I declare to you, today, if you will go into the cave with God, those things you've been praying and believing God for will begin to happen. Our society and the church need men who will bury themselves in Adullam and resurrect themselves to the new life "in Christ." The biggest challenge every one of us faces, male or female, is stepping into the cave and dying to self. Once you die to what you want, you will come alive to what God wants. Remember, if you make God first in your life, *"...all these other things will be added unto you"* (Matthew 6:33b).

We've discovered David was *wanted* both dead and alive.

He was on *God's Hit Man's List*, and so are you! Yes, you are wanted in this 21st century to be both dead and alive. No doubt about it—you are a *wanted man!*

CHAPTER FIVE

The Simplicity of Man's Success

Success defined by our 21st century society can seem hard to attain for many men. There are so many definitions of "success," it isn't any wonder so many are confused about it. Society has painted a picture that mega amounts of money or tremendous amounts of popularity mean success. However, in the Kingdom of God, *success is easy, failure is hard.* Success in the Kingdom of God is not defined by material possessions, professional accomplishments, educational achievements or bank accounts. There is a simplicity attached to success in the Kingdom of God. I want to show you how simple it is. In this chapter, I will give you some spiritual and practical instruction I hope will bless and challenge you at the same time. Even so, it will lead you to the success you have been longing for in your life.

As men, we must be acquainted with the fact that God has a simple plan on how we can be successful. It doesn't matter how old or young you are. It doesn't matter how many friends or contacts you have, how stylish or educated you are, who you know or what you know. All that matters is: success is simple! It is so simple that many times we overlook it because it's too easy.

I define success as the ability to fulfill the purpose for which God has assigned you in life. In other words, success is living your life on *purpose*—meaning: *You are successful if you are fulfilling your destiny by doing what God has assigned for you to do on this earth.* So, success for each man will be distinctive and will not look the same, since we all have a different assignment from God in life. If you try to be successful according to our society you may find yourself miserable and frustrated. The feeling of "failure" will overshadow you when you don't have a prosperous business, a thriving mega-church, or a big mansion with a nice Bentley parked in the garage. God wants you to experience success by being the best at what He has assigned you to do.

THE *GAP* CONCEPT

Let's take a look at what I like to call *The GAP Concept.* Ezekiel 22:30 says, *"And I sought for a man among them, that should make up the hedge, and stand in the gap before me for the land, that I should not destroy it: but I found none."* I shared this verse with you in the second chapter to show you that God's search for man wasn't a new thing; it is an old one. I explained to you that I believe God is simply looking for men who will rise and take their rightful place. We see God's search for man started with Adam. This leads me to another question: "What has God been trying to do since the beginning of time?" I believe God has been trying to show man the "simplicity of success." God has been trying to share His success secrets, principles, and formulas for centuries. He has made them available for us to use at anytime. God has been looking for men who have a desire to be a success—His way! Let's take another look at the beginning of time:

> And the LORD God planted a garden eastward
> in Eden; and there he put the man whom he
> had formed.

*And out of the ground made the LORD
God to grow every tree that is pleasant to the
sight, and good for food; the tree of life also
in the midst of the garden, and the tree of
knowledge of good and evil.*

*And a river went out of Eden to water
the garden; and from thence it was parted,
and became into four heads.*

*The name of the first is Pison: that is
it which compasseth the whole land of
Havilah, where there is gold;*

*And the gold of that land is good: there
is bdellium and the onyx stone.*

*And the name of the second river is
Gihon: the same is it that compasseth the
whole land of Ethiopia.*

*And the name of the third river is
Hiddekel: that is it which goeth toward the
east of Assyria. And the fourth river is
Euphrates.*

*And the LORD God took the man, and
put him into the garden of Eden to dress it
and to keep it.*

—Genesis 2:8-15

In this passage of Scripture, we discover God created a big world, but He had a strategic position especially designed for man. It was not an accident Adam was in the Garden of Eden. He was placed there on purpose. The word "Eden" is interpreted as the Delight of God. Eden can also be known as the "presence of God." I believe we can also say it was the place God delighted to be. God planted man where His presence dwelled and where He was abiding. Therefore, not only did God delight to be in Eden, He also enjoyed having man in Eden with Him. In other words, God put Adam in a

God-appointed place. This was the place where God and Adam could commune and fellowship together. Adam walked with the Lord in the cool of the morning on a daily basis where the Lord was able to give him the prescription or the directive for the day. Not only could Adam enjoy fellowship, but it was a place where God could resource Adam.

I define the *GAP* as the God-Appointed Place. What does it mean to stand in the GAP? It means spending time with God. Before the fall of Adam, that is exactly where he lived, in the *GAP*. The same relationship God had with Adam in Eden, is the same He desires with us today. God wants us to live in the place He delights! God wants you as a 21st century man to be in the God appointed place. We need to recognize that if we are not in the GAP, then God cannot fully utilize our lives the way He intended. The GAP is a necessary place which not only enables you to become acquainted with God and His ways, but also allows you to receive the vision and direction for your life. Do you not see success is what God envisioned for man from the beginning? God didn't set man up to fail!

It's very important for us to understand the GAP concept. It's important to know where God has positioned and placed us. It's important to know that if we are going to be used of the Lord then we have to be in the right place, at the right time and in the right setting in order to get the resources we need from the Lord. I also want you to understand this: *The man in the GAP is the man in the middle, who has the ability to make things happen.* Everything God has assigned you and I to do, everything we are accounted for doing in this life, if we stay in the *God-appointed place*, then we can receive everything we need from the Lord to do what God has assigned us to do.

Adam lived a successful life while he was fulfilling the

purpose for which he was created. As long as he was spending time with God and dressing and keeping the garden, he was a success. Adam chose the route of failure when he disobeyed God and moved out of the GAP. That was when failure entered the world. He had a choice of success or failure, just like you and I do today. We, as men, must recognize that a man's authority, a man's power, a man's ability to prosper emanates from being in the presence of God. Our decisions and the freewill that God gave us allows us to fail or succeed in life. It is true, the choices you make in life determine whether you will be successful at fulfilling your destiny.

THE SUCCESS PRINCIPLE

You may ask, "Bishop, how are you successful?" (I am glad you asked). Here is the success principle I use:

> *"Blessed is the man that walketh not in the counsel of the ungodly, nor standeth in the way of sinners, nor sitteth in the seat of the scornful. But his delight is in the law of the LORD; and in his law doth he meditate day and night. And he shall be like a tree planted by the rivers of water, that bringeth forth his fruit in his season; his leaf also shall not wither; and whatsoever he doeth shall prosper."*
>
> —Psalm 1:1-3

That's it! It sounds too simple, doesn't it? I am successful and fulfilled because I apply the principles in God's Word and allow them to be my navigation system in life. Or, in today's terms, I allow it to be my GPS. In essence, I allow God's Word to steer or manage the course of my life and lead me in the right direction. I allow it to be the delight of my life.. I delight in the "God of the Word" and also in doing the work God has assigned to me. God gives us insight, and if you capture this principle, you can get on the track to success.

THE SUPERNATURAL SUPPLY

Our delight as men should not always be in the NBA playoffs, the Super Bowl, our softball leagues or golf tournaments. Neither should our delight be in things where we feel a sense of accomplishment like our positions, our careers, our financial gains, nor our material possessions. Don't get me wrong. There is nothing wrong with the things I named, but the Bible shows us *our delight should be in the Lord.* To my young single brothers, your delight shouldn't be in how many phone numbers you have in your "little black book." *Your delight should be in the Lord.*

What is delight? Delight is what gives you enjoyment, makes you happy and leaves you feeling satisfied. Or, in other words, it is our pleasure or desire. Our pleasure should be in the law which is the Word of God. So, if the law is the Word and the Word was God and is God, then our delight should be in the presence of God (John 1:1). The Scripture also says, in His Word, or should I say, in His presence, we should meditate. This means we should ponder, imagine, and study His words. How often should we do this? I believe it says, "day and night." So, as a man, I can't become too busy living life that I miss time giving God His delight. Everything we need to fulfill the plan of God in this life will be found in His presence. Everything I need to take care of, such as my family and future generations, is in His presence. Everything God has planted in my spirit will be found when my delight is in His law, in His Word, in the GAP, which all represent His presence.

When you get in the presence of God something supernatural happens. The Psalmist said, *"We become like a tree planted by the rivers of water that brings forth fruit in our season"* (Psalm 1:3). Trees don't move; they are stable. They stay put. Our success comes from staying in the presence of God where we can hear what God is saying about our future. In His presence meditating, pondering, imagining and thinking is right where God resources us. He resources us by supplying and giving nourishment to our roots so we can bring forth fruit in our season. When God resources us, our leaves won't wither and whatever we touch shall prosper. Why? Because we have been in the presence of God, and in His presence we become like trees planted by the rivers of water.

THAT'S NOT FOR ME?

Most women really have no problem getting into the presence of God. They enjoy the presence of God and love to worship. It really doesn't take a whole lot for women. I notice this when our church has a Women's Conference. There is a jubilation and energy among the women, and it's not hard to get them to praise God. They are just plain excited about the things of God. Women love to worship whether it is private or public.

On the other hand, men struggle in this arena, privately and publicly. Spending sincere time alone with God seems to be a challenge that goes against our maleness. It goes against our hunter spirit and aggressive nature. Our nature is to conquer, to do something, to take control and to work with our hands. Some men desperately desire to be in the presence of God, but the feeling of having to do something overwhelms them. The feeling of having to use their hands, their skills and intellect, just seems to take over. Somewhere in a man's psyche is the concept of: "I can overcome, if I just get one more chance." Or, "If I just had the opportunity, I can make it happen." All the while, God is knocking on the door saying, "You sure can, but I need to tell you how to do it. I can't tell you how to do it until you slow down for a moment."

It is also a little harder for the man because the enemy works overtime to keep us from going into the presence of God. I reckon the reason he doesn't attack women is because he knows if he can cut off the male and keep him out of God's presence, he can put everything out of sync—EVERYTHING! He recognizes if we are cut off from our source of power, our source of authority, our source of inspiration, our source of ability, then the only thing we have left is our natural strength.

The average Christian man, today, is literally walking around operating in his own strength. We've abdicated our right to be able to come into the presence of God, because the enemy has caused God's presence to be viewed as something women do. Some men really do feel worship is a "female thing." The enemy has given men the mentality that men don't lift their hands to worship and men don't cry—leave it for the ladies. Men don't want to appear weak with their hands lifted in the air and tears rolling down their cheeks. So, their mentality is, *"That is not for me!"* This is one of the primary excuses the enemy gives men to keep them out of the presence of God. He makes men believe worship and being in the presence of God is all about emotionalism, which, by the way, is not true!

THE BUSY MAN'S SAGA

Another prime area the enemy uses to keep us out of the presence of God is *Busyness!* Most men are too busy handling their business. Even men who aren't doing anything, say they're busy. It's called *The Busy Man's Saga*. Many women testify to knowing men who aren't doing anything, but are constantly talking of how busy they are. Men say, "I've got to take care of this and that...I've got places to go and people to see...I've got stuff to do." Many women are standing by confused because they don't see any fruit from their man's busyness. They wonder, where is the evidence? When women want to know where the fruit is, most men can't even explain. Most men are usually five minutes behind schedule when they get up in the morning anyway. They usually start off their morning with the enemy either making them oversleep or telling them they are too busy to spend time with God.

Gentlemen, it is a strategic attack of the enemy to keep us cut off from our Source. It is a strategic attack to keep us disconnected from our supply of power and authority. Our ability to properly cultivate the gift of life comes from a priority of commitment to our time with the Creator. Jesus said, *"I have come that you might have life and life more abundantly"* (John 10:10b). How do we attain abundant life? How do we become a vehicle of blessing? How do we become a vehicle of prosperity? How do we become a conduit from which we can flow? You can't buy it, you can't earn it, nor can you find it. Abundant life comes when you delight in the presence of God. That is where the blessing comes from. I don't care how much overtime you work or how much money you obtain, you can't buy the blessing of God. I discovered when I stay in the presence of God, God has a way of opening up doors I didn't know existed, which is one of the blessings of God.

I want you to know how to get blessed and become confident providers and cultivators. Although, I have been sharing with you the simplicity of a man's success, you have to find a place where you can get in God's presence to receive daily instruction and wisdom. You have to say, "Lord, I need to hear from You today before I make a move or get too busy. Please give me guidance for the day."

My wife can testify on my behalf. It doesn't matter whether I'm in a hotel in Africa, California, or at home, when the morning comes, I'm in the GAP. I stay there listening for God to speak to me. When I didn't get in the GAP before beginning my daily activities, I felt like I walked out of my house and forgot to put my pants on. I also felt overwhelmed like something was wrong or out of place. It was not a good feeling. If I don't get in the GAP, how can I effectively minister to my wife and children, my congregation or anyone else I come in contact with? I have to ask God, what is the prescription for the day? As I encounter my daily activities, I am then greeted with success, because God is with me and my destiny is being fulfilled.

CONSISTENCY: THE KEY TO SUCCESS

Consistency is the key to your success and victories in life. It is very important to understand that the thing that will make you head and shoulders above other men is consistently delighting in the Word and being in the GAP. Please understand, being in and enjoying the presence of God is not seasonal! We don't obtain seasonal passes like we do at amusement parks, such as Busch Gardens, King's Dominion, or Six Flags. You can't delight in God and be in the GAP this week and not the next. You can't love God this month, and next month He's wondering who you are because He hasn't heard from you until you are in trouble. Your success lies in your consistency. There has to be a commitment where you are willing to submit your time to God, seven days a week.

Second Chronicles 26:1-4 gives a good illustration of how

consistency is key to your success. Uzziah was sixteen years old when he became king. He tapped into the secret of success at a young age. He was able to rebuild Elath and restore it after Amaziah died. The Bible says, *"... He did what was right in the eyes of the Lord...He sought God during the days of Zechariah, who instructed him in the fear of God. As long as he sought the Lord, God gave him success."* His success is attributed to being in the *God-appointed place* and consistently seeking the face of God. We, too, are guaranteed success when we consistently seek the face of God and walk in our destiny.

THE 24/31 CHALLENGE

As a man, husband, father, brother, uncle, friend and pastor, I have been challenged. Challenge is what has taken my manhood to new dimensions I never knew existed. It has taken my life to a place of blessing. As a pastor, I yearn for the men in my congregation to be flourishing, successful, and blessed. Not only do I want to see men in my church blessed, I also want to see you, the reader, blessed. I desire to see you become a man of divine destiny. So, I challenge you. For some, the challenge won't seem hard enough and for others it will be one of the most difficult things you've ever done in your life. When God birthed the **24/31 Challenge** in my spirit, He spoke to my heart and said He desired to make powerful men of God. These are the words He spoke to me:

> "Preacher, the only way they can become powerful men is to stop being so busy and give Me some time. You can't preach it into them, you can't pray it into them, and you can't force it into them. They have to come to Me freely. If they come freely and give me 24 minutes, I will speak to them and make myself

real to them. I will begin to give them wisdom, and I will be able to give them My plan. I will begin to share with them opportunities and secret paths. I will begin to open up windows for them that they didn't know existed. I will begin to show them how to do what they have been trying to do for the last five, ten, fifteen, and twenty years. I will show them how to make it happen. But, I have to know that they're not leaning on their own understanding, but are willing to acknowledge Me in all of their ways."

By now, you are familiar with Psalm 1:2 from the Bible. I want to share my interpretation of this verse with you: *"But his delight is in the GAP. His delight is in the presence of the Lord and in His presence does he meditate day and night"* (Bishop Francisco Version). If you believe there is something else left for you to do on this earth, if you believe God has some things He wants you to overtake and take control of, if you believe there is something God wants you to do for your family and future generations that you haven't done yet, or if there is something you've been working hard to accomplish and it hasn't happened yet—*accept my challenge!* Delight in Him! If you know on the inside, without a shadow of a doubt God wants to do something in and through you, I want you to take this verse and accept my challenge.

Here is the challenge I gave to the men in my congregation and now am presenting to you. The challenge was for men to take the next thirty-one days of their life and give God a tithe of their time. Do I have you wondering about the tithe of time? Just like we give God a tenth of our increase (money), I am asking you to give God a tenth of your time. A true tithe of your time is approximately two hours and forty minutes because there are twenty-four hours in a day. However, I'm not asking you for this much time. I know this is a big step for some men. So, I'm asking you to give God 24 minutes per day for the next 31 consecutive days. Gentlemen, this includes Friday and Sunday which means you can't skip a day and pick back up where you left off. If you miss a day then you have to start back at *Day One*.

If you accept the challenge, 24 minutes for 31 consecutive days, it will begin to give you insight into the benefits and the blessings of God upon your life, your family and everything you set your hands to accomplish. Remember, God is seeking to share His wisdom and His plans with someone. He is seeking for someone who wants to be blessed. He is waiting to show men where the opportunities are for themselves and their seed's seed. God is looking for a man who is ready to take His *SUPER* and put it with his *natural* to produce supernatural results in this world. God wants you to live the successful life He planned for you.

HOW IT WORKS

Here is the formula I would like for you to follow during this challenge. I want you to spend 12 minutes in the morning and 12 minutes at night or 24 minutes total alone with God. It's your choice of how you want to do it. However, there are some other conditions I would like to present to you, such as: no cell phone, no pager, no TV, no radio, no computer, and no interruptions—just you alone with God. This will allow you to be isolated with no interruptions (like David was in the cave of Adullam). If you would like to use a stopwatch or timer to assist you during this time, that is fine. The most important thing is that you spend quality time alone with God. All I want you to do during this time is simply invite God in and just listen.

Gentlemen, you don't have to invite your wife to assist you in prayer because you don't think you know how to pray. That's alright! You don't have to know how to pray. I don't care if you don't see any lightning flashes, hear any thunder, feel anything or if you cry or don't cry—it's alright! It's not about emotions. I just want you to get acquainted with the presence of God without thinking about your job, your problems, your cat, your goldfish, or your next golf tournament. I want you to focus your attention on Him. Your attitude must be, "God, this is Your time and for the next twelve minutes, I want to think and meditate according to Psalm 1:2-3. I want to meditate upon You, Lord. God, I need You to speak to me." Let God speak to you and whatever He says to you, you just listen. After you listen, then is the time to ask the Father to speak to you about your children, your wife, your career, your future, and so forth. It's the time to ask God to speak to you about yourself and the things He wants to do in your life. Above all, don't feel like you have to come out of the *GAP* to accomplish anything great—only do what God tells you to do.

God's heart desire is to see men be like trees planted by the rivers of water. Trees don't grow overnight. Have you ever seen a tree grow? When did it happen? You don't know. You don't have any recollection of when the tree grew so big. It seems one day it was just big. When did it grow? It grew little by little by little. Here a little and there a little. We grow line upon line, precept upon precept by the Word and presence of God. Give God a tithe of time. Spend the 12 minutes in the morning and evening, 24 minutes for 31 days alone with God, seeking His face with no interruptions. You will see the true value of time well spent with God.

I don't want to be blessed by myself. My desire is to see other men become successful and fulfill their destinies in life. As I've shared, it will only come by being in the presence of God. I believe this 31 day challenge will launch you into another dimension of your life. Success is just waiting to happen in your life!

24 MINUTES PER DAY + 31 CONSECUTIVE DAYS = A BRAND NEW MAN

CHAPTER SIX

A Good Daddy

One of the most misunderstood roles of a man in our times is the role of a father. Somehow, in our society, fatherhood has become a position of little or no significance at all. There is a generation of young men longing for examples of fatherhood, while another generation of men are wondering, 'what happened to fatherhood?' Yes, fatherhood is included in the war on man's identity and is an area we must fight hard to reclaim for ourselves and our children. While many men may not understand the true significance or see the value of their role as a father, in the sight of their child's eyes, their role as a father is one of the most prominent positions in the world. Proverbs 17:6 says, *"Children's children are the crown of old men; and the glory of children are their fathers."* You are the glory of your children.

Many times as we look back in our history at our fathers, grandfathers and great grandfathers, we see how their actions have caused either blessing or cursing in our family line today. We must understand that as men, we define by example what happens in our household. In other words, the examples we set are what the next generation will look like. It is the intergenerational power passed from generation to generation that I spoke of briefly in the first chapter. We have an opportunity as men to define what's going to happen in the next generation. You have a chance right now to influence and define how your son or daughter will treat their children.

THINK GENERATIONALLY

You must be aware of the influence and tremendous power which resides in you. If you are an absentee father, an abusive father or a devout father, you set in place for future generations to be absentee, abusive or devout fathers. If you are a hard worker, you set a standard, and your son or daughter will see hard work is essential and you will have produced hard workers. If you are lazy and excuse laden, you will more than likely produce lazy and excuse laden children. If you sit at home while your woman goes to work and your sons see momma putting bread on the table, what have you produced? Your son is going to grow up searching for a woman to take care of him. They are following the example you set as a father. Please understand this because you set the tone for the quality of life your family will experience. You are the one who makes the difference in their lives.

As a father, you have a responsibility to think "generationally." You have to think about leaving a legacy for your children. *"A good man leaves an inheritance for his children's children..."* (Proverbs 13:22). I am not just referring to money, but a legacy of love, faith, wisdom, good work ethic, good examples, etc. Men, we cannot afford to live for the moment with our minds only on what we want. There are too many lives at stake. It's not about us, but about our seed which is our children and their children. You are on this earth for a short time; what will you contribute? Do you ever stop and wonder what will happen to your loved ones when you are gone? There are choices I could have made in life, but I decided a long time ago that life wasn't just about me. I had to ponder some hard questions: Do I sell out to get everything my heart desires so that I am happy and everyone else is in hell and miserable? Or, do I understand that my responsibility and role as a man is to make the kind of choices that will impact the lives of others in a positive way?

I discovered years ago the more you make an impact in the lives of others, the more God will bless your life. In all actuality, life is more about those assigned to you. If we can comprehend this fact, then we can recognize what it means to be a male, a man, a father, or a husband. It brings us to our significance of being a man who understands his ability to impact generations and be blessed at the same time.

BECOMING A GOOD DADDY

The terminology of daddy implies one who has fathered or one who has begotten a child. This directly relates to the male parent. It's easy to bash men about what they are not doing, especially in the times in which we live. However, my goal is to share the traits of a good daddy and encourage you to be one. You know I am not referring to you being a "sugar daddy" or a "sweet daddy," right? I'm talking about a good daddy to your children.

Malachi 4:5-6 says: *"Behold, I will send you Elijah the prophet before the coming of the great and dreadful day of the LORD: And he shall turn the heart of the fathers to the children, and the heart of the children to their fathers, lest I come and smite the earth with a curse."* God in this particular passage of Scripture allows us to see the importance of the father. A biological father who does not fulfill his role as father, literally becomes one of satan's devices to upset God's plan for a healthy and well-balanced society. A biological father who does not take his rightful place becomes a tool the enemy can use. I was fascinated by an article I read several years ago in a *Family Times* magazine which could attest to this. It stated:

> "...almost 25 million children are living apart from their biological fathers. 40% of these have never seen their fathers in at least one year. 60% have never even set foot in their father's home. Every year 1 million children are born to unwed parents while another 1 million are newly affected by divorce. In addition to this, there are estimated to be 6 million children who have fathers who are physically present, but emotionally absent—withholding time, nurture and love."

The article also stated, "...these children are more likely on average to be poor, to fail in school, especially the boys because they lack a positive male example in their life, they are more inclined to have health, emotional and psychological problems. They are more inclined to be victims of child abuse, die of AIDS or engage in violence or criminal behavior, more so than their peers who live with married biological fathers."

I believe the crisis we face in this 21st century is a crisis of ignorance. Hosea 4:6 says, *"My people are destroyed for lack of knowledge..."* Many males simply don't understand what it means to be a father. Or, should I say, "A good daddy." They have no concept of what it means to be a father figure who nurtures his children. Many men relish and take pride in the fact that they can produce a child, but lack the ability to care and provide for the child. What constitutes a good daddy is the ability to love, nurture and be involved in your child's life. If these dynamics are missing then men are not daddies; they are sperm donors.

There are many males who have the ability to contribute sperm, but lack the ability to take care of what they have created. (Every male is not a man. They may be male, but they haven't developed into manhood.) I want you to get a clear-cut picture of what you are like if you are a sperm donor. You are like an organ donor who after giving up his organ, dies. The organ donor has left a contribution, but is no longer there. I know it seems harsh, but it is the same concept when you give life to someone, but you are not available to care for the life. As I said before, my focus is not to bash fathers, whether they be good, bad, AWOL, or part-time fathers. I just want you to see what you look like if this pertains to you.

As a father, I want to encourage those who currently are and those who will become fathers in the future. I don't want to give the impression that I am a man who has all the answers on what it means to be a father or one who knows how to do it perfectly—*I don't!* Now, if you would have asked me fifteen years ago, I may possibly have told you I had the answers. I remember preaching sermons on "the family" fifteen years ago where I really thought I had answers. I really thought if individuals would do things a particular way, then everything in their family would be alright. Nevertheless, time has taught me, although sincere, I was sincerely wrong! One of my greatest discoveries was learning that you can't package and distribute what it takes to be a good father. There is no package, DVD set, brochure, computer program or book you can buy to give you *all* the answers about raising your children. It doesn't work that way! You will find every child and home is different, just like every marriage and situation is different. It takes willingness, will-power, and a whole lot of work! It means you have to put forth the effort to do what is necessary in order to become a good daddy. There are four traits which make a good daddy:

A GOOD DADDY KNOWS HIS CHILDREN

Bishop, how do you know a good daddy knows his children? God told the prophet Jeremiah, *"...before I formed thee in the belly, I knew thee"* (Jeremiah 1:5). If our Heavenly Father knows us and is the epitome and perfect example of fatherhood, then every man should model or emulate himself after God. As men, we have the responsibility to follow God's example of fatherhood to know our children as well.

A tremendous part of being an effective father is knowing your children. Effective fathers know the temperament of their children. They know what motivates them, what makes them different, what makes them happy and what makes them sad. They know their hurts, their fears, their joys, their pleasures, their strengths and their weaknesses. You have to recognize whether your child is an extrovert or an introvert, whether they like the limelight or prefer being in the background, whether they are encouragers or need more encouraging. It is the responsibility of the father to identify where his children are. An effective father (a good daddy) studies to know his children. He is not absent without leave (AWOL). He is not a father who comes home, grabs a remote or gets on the internet and doesn't have any interaction with his children. A good daddy is willing to work at studying his children so he will know them.

As a father, you have to develop the ability to discern and know when your child has a difficult day. I want you to stop and think about how you feel when you have a bad day. Think about how you like individuals to respond to you on your bad day. We all have bad days, including our children. What if somebody told you on your bad day to take that frown off your face and suck it up? Be honest, you wouldn't like it. Why do it to your children? Why tell them to go to their rooms, remove the frown from their face or else...? A good daddy knows whether or not his child is upset from having a difficult day and takes an interest in the events of their day. These are things I have learned over the years about being a good daddy.

There are two reasons fathers should aggressively pursue knowledge about their children and want to know more about them. The first is to be able to help create conditions in which they can grow. As a father, it is my responsibility to produce an environment where I understand the unique personality of my child which will enable them to grow and flourish. I must create an environment which encourages them to be who they are and not who I want them to be.

Many fathers try to live their lives through their sons. You want your son to be a superstar football player because you didn't cut it. It is the reason you push your son so hard. You are making him become the superstar football player because you missed your opportunity to become one. You thought you should have gone to the NFL, but because you didn't, you are putting unnecessary pressure on your son to become a pro athlete. Fathers, we can't do this to our boys. If we do this, we harm them instead of help them. In order to produce an environment where they can flourish, we have to accept them for who they are. Your child might not be a football player; they might be a rocket scientist. While you are trying to get them to throw the ball, they are trying to shoot to the moon. Please don't impose your lost dreams on your children; they deserve a chance to be what God ordained them to be.

I have three daughters who have three unique and different personalities. I knew one of my daughters was going to be very outgoing. I paid attention to the particular things she loved doing at a very young age. One of her favorite activities was playing dress-up. She loved to prance around, especially in the evening when I came home from work. She would walk around in her mother's high heel shoes or anything else she could find. Her mother and I would participate in her little fashion show by playing along with her. I played along as her announcer. I would say, "Here we have our lovely model coming in; she is modeling a wonderful hat and beautiful shoes." She would eat it up! If I did this for my other daughters, they would say, "Come on dad, what are you doing?" My point is, you've got to understand your children. You've got to know them and understand what is unique about their personality. Then, as a father, it is your responsibility to create conditions in which they can grow. You have to create the kind of soil in which they can produce and thrive.

The second reason a father should know his children is to recognize danger signals in their lives. It is the male's responsibility to know his children and be able to recognize danger signals in their lives. It is for you to know when they need intervention and guidance. We should be able to pick up in the spirit realm and sense when problems are present in their lives. If some are present, we should pull them to the side to ask, "Is everything ok?" They need to know daddy is going to be the one who will always protect them and provide for them. They need to understand you are more than their provider; you are genuinely concerned about their lives.

It doesn't matter whether you physically live with your children or not. A good daddy knows his children. I am aware we have situations in this 21st century where fathers are separated for various reasons and can't live with their children. However, it doesn't mean you have the right to abdicate the responsibilities God assigned to you. You still need to know your child. You still need to be interactive and participate in your child's life. Letting your child know they have someone concerned about them is being a good daddy. They need to know they have a father, a male component who is concerned about their life.

A GOOD DADDY VALUES HIS CHILDREN

Back to Malachi 4:6, God promises, *"...he shall turn the heart of the fathers to the children, and the heart of the children to their fathers..."* You may wonder, "How will the children's hearts be turned to the fathers? How will children begin to look up to men again? How will children begin to respect the male component? How will children begin to honor the father once again?" The Bible is literally telling us that children will honor the father when the father honors them, meaning: When fathers' hearts are turned to their children, and they place worth and value in being in their children's lives, *then* their children will relish and look up to them. But, men who don't give their children time and attention shouldn't expect their children to look up to them. If your children become rebellious and begin to give you grief and bitterness, I believe they are seeking your attention. If they begin to bring shame and disgrace, they are saying, "I want you to be involved in my life." If you prove your children are a priority in your life, they will honor and respect you. God wants to do a new thing which will cause men to turn their hearts towards their children and their children towards them. It will happen as you begin to invest into the lives of your children. As you do, they will have a change of heart and will see you with eyes of love, honor, and respect.

A pediatrician named Dr. Barry Brazelton (in the article I referred to earlier) said, "Everything we know shows that when men are involved with their children, the child's IQ increases by the time they are 6 or 7. The child is more likely to have a sense of humor, to develop an inner-excitement to believe in himself or herself and to be more motivated to learn."

Please think about this: *Fatherhood is a one time shot!* You only get one shot per child. You get one opportunity to be a father. You get one opportunity to speak into your child's life. You can't go back and redo it. There are no rewind buttons to push in life when we make mistakes. No matter how much you would like to, it's not possible. It may be 20 or 30 years down the road when a light bulb comes on and you say, "I wish..." But, it's too late! Please don't fool yourself; it's a one shot opportunity. I believe the degree of success we have with our children is directly linked to the personal involvement we have in their lives at an early age. Some men expect and accept the fact that their role in the family is one of a provider. They believe if they provide shelter for their children, put food on the table, and clothes on their backs then their job is complete. The philosophy of some men is that women ought to be nurturers while they are hunters. That is why when a child hurts their finger or falls down and has an accident, men say, "Go see your momma!" But, if we truly understand what it means to be a parent, we know it's not *all* momma's responsibility to care for the children. Fathers must also be intricately involved in the life of their sons and daughters so they can develop holistically. Your son and your daughter need your time, attention and affection. You have a responsibility to take an active part in your children's lives. You can't continue to sit on the side and expect mothers to do all the work. You have to become involved before it's too late.

To men who are new fathers or soon to be fathers, the little child you hold on your lap or lay in the crib or the baby soon to arrive, is a God-given gift. The child you have been divinely blessed with will need three things from you: time, attention, and affection. They are going to need you to support them at school assemblies, church events, academic efforts, extracurricular activities, sporting events, playtime, etc. They are going to need you to show them some affections which break you out of your comfort zone and allows them to see the real you. They need this! Your father may have never told you he loved you, but your child needs to hear that you love him or her. Make no mistake about it, they need to hear this from you! If you don't tell them you love them, somebody else will. Somebody else who tells them they love them may not truly love them. This may cause great harm to your child. They need to experience the genuine love of a father who loves them unconditionally and accepts them for who they are. That's the function of the father today.

A good daddy values his relationship with his children and is willing to make the necessary investments in their lives. Whether it be emotional, spiritual, physical, or financial, he wants to invest and bless the lives of his children. Your responsibility as a father (and mine) is to produce well-balanced children who know how to cope effectively with the perplexities of this life.

As a father, it's my responsibility to teach my daughters how to be balanced in an unbalanced world. It's my responsibility to teach my children how to deal in a unfair world. It's my responsibility to teach them how to be leaders and not followers in a society which tries to pull them down. It's my responsibility to teach them everything will not always go their way. They must be aware of how to deal with difficult times and know how to work through them. I must teach them to face their giants instead of run away from them. It's my responsibility and yours to teach and develop children who will add to society and not become a detriment to society.

Statistics tell us when fathers don't take their rightful roles, many times our children (especially boys) are set up for failure. Most of the individuals in prison are men who didn't have father figures in their homes. So, it's our responsibility to make sure we develop children who know how to deal with situations and complexities of life. It doesn't mean we always step up to take the heat. Sometimes we step behind and say, "I got your back, but you've got to deal with this one." It's part of teaching them. I teach my children all the time and they don't even know I am teaching them life lessons.

I flipped the script when my oldest daughter was moving into her new apartment for college. I had her call Virginia Power to get her utilities turned on. I had her call the sanitation, the water works department, insurance company and all the other places she needed to call. I could have done it, but I let her do it. You may ask, why? But, I ask you, "How am I helping her if I do everything for her?" She didn't know I was teaching her another level of adulthood. She also didn't know the next level of adulthood I would teach her was how to pay her own rent. You teach them subtly. You find lessons which challenge and encourage them to take on the responsibilities of life. Many times we raise children in our society to be dependent on their parents. It is the reason 30 and 40 year olds are moving back home or have never left home at all. Teach them the responsibilities of life. Don't try to shield and protect them from everything. Good daddies prepare their children to deal with the realities of life.

A GOOD DADDY PROVIDES A HOME

Genesis 18:19 says, *"For I know him, that he will command his children and his household after him, and they shall keep the way of the LORD, to do justice and judgment; that the LORD may bring upon Abraham that which he hath spoken of him."* God was speaking about Abraham when He said, *"I know him..."* God knew Abraham would command, constitute, and charge his children and household to follow after Him. He knew Abraham would be a man who would lead his home. Daddy, it is your responsibility to make sure your children follow after you and don't lead you. I know I may hit a nerve; however, your son shouldn't be playing Nintendo while you are outside cutting the grass. You have to teach your boys how to take on some responsibilities. I know you think they are "all of that," but you still need to let them push the lawn mower, pull weeds, take the trash out, vacuum the car, wash dishes and so forth, even if they try to put a guilt trip on you. It's part of providing a home.

Good daddies provide a home not just a house. There is a difference between providing a house and a home. A good daddy works at providing a home that produces an atmosphere of peace and tranquility, so when his children come home, they don't come into a cold house. They come into a place of peace and tranquility. It is also the responsibility of the father not to come into his house using intimidation tactics, saying, "I'm the man of this house!" Your presence ought to speak. Peace and tranquility ought to come over the home rather than fear and trepidation. There should be a "Daddy's home and no matter what happens we are going to be alright" atmosphere. It is comforting and makes a difference to know your presence brings a peace over your home and makes things better.

Fathers have to carefully monitor their home life, meaning: the way you treat your wife matters. Children instinctively and intuitively pick up on the temperament of the home. I grew up in a home where I didn't see my mother and father constantly bickering and arguing. If they did, it was out of our sight. I never heard my mother or father put the other down. Our home was peaceful. My father set the tone by the way he treated my mother.

Daddies are the barometer, not mommies. You are the barometer who sets the temperature of the house. You determine whether things will be hot, cold, balanced, unbalanced, peaceful or chaotic in your house. What kind of temperature do you set in your home? It's the male's responsibility to monitor his home. Home should be a safe haven, a place of refuge and relaxation where everyone can let their hair down and not walk around on eggshells. I don't walk around my home afraid. I don't walk around my home intimidated nor do I want my children to do so. I want them to be free. As a matter of fact, sometimes they're too free. Anyone of my children, at any given moment, will come flop in my lap while I am reclined in my La-Z-Boy. It is the atmosphere I created for my home. I love it, because I am their daddy, and they are comfortable with me. I vowed to protect and care for my daughters. I want them to know there is not another male who loves them the way I do. I want them to understand I am always available for them. If I had a son, I would do the same thing. I would show love to my sons. I would constantly express my love and desire to have a healthy relationship with them.

Referring back to the relationship between God and Abraham, God knew Abraham would set the tone for his house. As a result, God didn't withhold anything from him. In essence, God was saying, when a man sets the tone for his house, I will bless him with everything he needs to be a blessing to his home. God will bless the father who takes care of his family and business. God will bless you when you make sure there is an atmosphere of love, peace, provision, protection, play and promotion in the household. It's not all about discipline. Children need discipline, but there is more to fathering than that. You must be able to keep the peace, be actively involved, and discipline when necessary. It has been taboo for men to be involved in the life of their children because we are trying to uphold a macho image. *But, at home, you need to be daddy!* At home, you need to be able to show and express love.

Some of my fondest memories of my daughters are sitting on the floor wrestling with them. I enjoyed them, and they enjoyed me. I remember all three of them ganging up on me. I had a blast letting them think they had gotten the best of daddy.

Dads, you have to find unique and creative ways to interact with your children. Whether it may be biking, playing a game, going on an outing, going out to lunch, or throwing rocks in a pond, don't allow your children to watch television all day or play Nintendo DS, Xbox 360, PlayStation 3, Wii and all the latest video games; it's a chance to create lifetime memories. If they are hooked, wean them off by spending quality time with them.

Fathers, invest early in the life of your children. Invest in their younger years if you want to be significant in their later years. Anything you can do to spend time with your children while they are young will benefit both of you. You have about ten years to develop a relationship with them. Once they are older than ten years old, if you haven't developed a relationship with them, it's going to be very, very difficult. They need you to interact with them during those precious years. They need you to spend time and be a major part of their lives. The home should be a place where your child longs to return and be a part. Now is the time to establish fond memories as part of their lives, which will indelibly mark their minds. They need to remember lovely, wonderful, and beautiful things about their home and about you. You don't have to spend a whole lot of money to make this happen—just time, attention, and affection.

YOU SHOULD HONOR A GOOD DADDY

If you have a good daddy then you need to honor him. Make sure you give him the love and respect he is due. Make sure you bless him by letting him know you appreciate his life. A man needs to be affirmed and needs to hear his life matters in yours. He needs to know you appreciate him and all he has done. Children should honor their fathers and mothers, no matter how old they are. If your father has or is providing a home, food, clothing as well as the other needs in your life, then you need to honor your father and esteem him. Let your children witness you honoring *your dad*. Remember, you are establishing how they will treat you.

Fatherhood is not an easy task. There are many demands and expectations that people place on fathers. You frequently hear, "You ought to do this," and "you ought to do that..." I want to say to you, *"Do what God assigned you to do."* Love your child. Give them time, attention, and affection and you will receive the respect and honor you deserve as a daddy from your family.

Fathers are the progenitors of life, which ultimately means we are responsible for life. Let us take our proper places and turn our hearts toward our children by nurturing, loving, and honoring them as God's gift to us. You hear mothers say all the time, "My son...my daughter...my child." It is not just the mother's child. If daddy wasn't there, no child would be. It is the father's responsibility to take ownership of his children, speak into their lives and build loving relationships with them.

Well, Bishop, what if my father isn't or never was in the picture? I believe God has placed someone in your life who can be a father figure. It may be a man at your church, at the local grocery store, on your job, or in your neighborhood.

You may not recognize him. Pay attention to the man who takes an interest in your well-being. The one who is concerned about you becoming better and being the best you, is God-sent. There are positive male role models all around you who can speak into your life and be a good example for you. (We will discuss this in more detail in the next chapter.) As you grow, you will be able to bless the lives of your family and speak into the lives of other brothers who were in your same situation.

My father left home at the age of twelve. He didn't have a father figure. He didn't have anyone to speak into his life. But he turned around his negative situation and raised the family he didn't have. I think we turned out pretty well. I want to say to you, just because you have or had a negative situation does not mean you can't take it and turn it around. Look at the bright side: at least you know what not to do.

BLENDING FAMILIES

I want to encourage men who God has called to step into a very challenging role of fatherhood. I stated earlier that, "fatherhood is not an easy task." It is even more challenging when you are blending families together. The times we live in require some men to take care of not only their natural children, but other children who have been entrusted into their keep. Blended families are something we have grown accustomed to and have become the norm in the 21st century. I believe it takes a man with a special call on his life to be able to father children who are not his own. It is a special call when you can love, provide for and protect as your own, a child who is not from your own loins. When you make a conscious decision to show them the God kind of love and show them what God wants to do in their life, you have set yourself up for God's blessing in your life. Never be ashamed that God chose you to be the head of a blended family—you can be a good daddy!

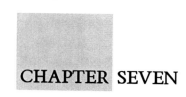

CHAPTER SEVEN

The Need for a Mentor

We have discussed the various issues a 21st century man must face and seen how the responsibilities of everyday life can be very demanding. This "demand" has placed many men on the verge of exhaustion. They are facing the ongoing epidemic of "burn-out." They are burning themselves out and everyone else around them. Some are so tired they are at the point of throwing in the towel. In this chapter, I want you to see that you don't have to give up, quit, retreat, or throw in the towel. You just might be at a point in your life where you need a good mentor.

I believe what is lacking in the lives of a lot of 21st century men is *mentorship*. Yes, there seems to be a deficiency in mentorship being received and given. You may at this point ask me: What is a mentor and who needs one? First, I will tell you every man needs one. One of the most valuable things a man can have in his life is a mentor. Second, a mentor is a trusted someone who looks out for your best interest and communicates life skills and principles. A mentor is someone who shares their wisdom, guidance, and experiences with you, for your good. Mentors are individuals who shake us out of our complacency, hold us accountable, ask hard questions others are not willing to ask and give advice that may be hard to digest. A good mentor will propel you into your destiny. When we receive a mentor into our lives we experience benefits such as: protection, strength, accountability, counsel, friendship, direction, correction, and encouragement. Sounds like something every man needs, right?

YOU CAN'T DO IT ALONE!

A perfect illustration of why men need mentors in their life is found in Exodus 18:12-27:

> *"And Jethro, Moses' father in law, took a burnt offering and sacrifices for God: and Aaron came, and all the elders of Israel, to eat bread with Moses' father in law before God. And it came to pass on the morrow, that Moses sat to judge the people: and the people stood by Moses from the morning unto the evening. And when Moses' father in law saw all that he did to the people, he said, What is this thing that thou doest to the people? why sittest thou thyself alone, and all the people stand by thee from morning unto even? And Moses said unto his father in law, Because the people come unto me to enquire of God: When they have a matter, they come unto me; and I judge between one and another, and I do make them know the statutes of God, and his laws. And Moses' father in law said unto him, The thing that thou doest is not good. Thou wilt surely wear away, both thou, and this people that is with thee: for this thing is too heavy for thee; thou art not able to perform it thyself alone. Hearken now unto my voice, I will give thee counsel, and God shall be with thee: Be thou for the people to God-ward, that thou mayest bring the causes unto God: And thou shalt teach them ordinances and laws, and shalt shew them the way wherein they must walk, and the work that they must do. Moreover thou shalt*

provide out of all the people able men, such as fear God, men of truth, hating covetousness; and place such over them, to be rulers of thousands, and rulers of hundreds, rulers of fifties, and rulers of tens: And let them judge the people at all seasons: and it shall be, that every great matter they shall bring unto thee, but every small matter they shall judge: so shall it be easier for thyself, and they shall bear the burden with thee. If thou shalt do this thing, and God command thee so, then thou shalt be able to endure, and all this people shall also go to their place in peace. So Moses hearkened to the voice of his father in law, and did all that he had said. And Moses chose able men out of all Israel, and made them heads over the people, rulers of thousands, rulers of hundreds, rulers of fifties, and rulers of tens. And they judged the people at all seasons: the hard causes they brought unto Moses, but every small matter they judged themselves. And Moses let his father in law depart; and he went his way into his own land."

I believe this passage points out a truth most men miss: *"You're not alone and you can't do it alone!"* Everybody needs somebody. Although Moses was a great leader and had an intimate relationship with God where he spoke directly to Him on various occasions, he was yet vulnerable. Certain areas in this great leader's life needed the assistance, counsel and wisdom of another human being. So, God sent Moses' father-in-law, Jethro, to mentor and speak into his life.

WHAT'S THE PROBLEM?

The problem was: *Moses was stuck!* He was entrenched in what he had always done. Many times we get stuck in our own methodology which causes us to end up in a rut. It happens when we feel something is working, we've always done it like this and it appears to be the "right thing" to do. Moses may have felt he had a flawless system established. He may have thought he had a perfect flow. He soon found out he didn't. When Jethro confronted Moses and informed him that what he was doing was not a "good thing" and neither he nor his people would last, he challenged Moses to make a paradigm shift. (A *paradigm* is something that is an accepted action, system or method of doing things that has become normal.) Jethro showed Moses what the problem was: God never meant for him to be a "super pastor." His current judicial methods were madness. He was exhausting himself and his people. He was putting unnecessary pressure on himself. He was stifling the leadership ability of capable men among him. God used Jethro to help Moses change from what had been a normal accepted practice to a better way.

If you are stuck in your present way of doing things, God may be calling you to do something different. *And*, He may send a mentor or someone with just the advice or wisdom you need. There is always a better way to do things and sometimes we can't differentiate it by ourselves. Most times, it won't be a "voice from heaven," it will be a "Jethro" who shows you a "more excellent way." Sometimes we feel something is working and see no need for change—period. After all, it's always worked before, and it's the way it's always been done, right? I believe God wants us to realize there is always a better way of doing and approaching things.

Sometimes it takes an outsider to help us make a paradigm shift, so we don't remain in the same situation. Moses was surrounded by capable men who feared God, hated covetousness, had good judgment and were full of integrity. However, it took a mentor to show him what his problem was. God sent him a mentor to teach him about strategy and delegating authority. (A good mentor will not only show you your problems, he will also give solutions.) Isn't it wonderful to know we don't always have to have the answers? It should be refreshing to know we don't always have to execute things the same way it has always been done because there is a better way! Sometimes we don't recognize it, yet a good mentor will.

THE KEYS TO RECEIVING MENTORSHIP

One of the keys to receiving "mentorship" is found in a man's willingness to *be receptive.* He has to be prepared to move out of the confinement of his "little box" by being open to suggestions. If Moses rejected the wisdom of his father-in-law because he thought of him as family and felt he was "too familiar" with him, he couldn't have fulfilled his God-given assignment. He wouldn't have been able to move forward. He would have continued to suppress his growth as well as the capable leaders who were among him.

Mentors are not "one-size fits all," meaning: Your mentor may not look like you think he should. He may come from a different background or ethnicity than you (like Jethro). He may be someone you've been acquainted with for years (like Jethro) or someone you've just met. He may hold a MBA or PhD or he may not have even graduated from high school. A well-known axiom states, "Never judge a book by its cover." Judging a person based on their outward appearance can fool many and you can miss out on one of the biggest blessings of your life. Don't box yourself in; be receptive and discerning to who God is sending to help take your life to the next level.

Humility is another key to receiving mentorship. We are never too old, anointed, or knowledgeable not to receive mentoring.

A person's counsel and wisdom might just be what we need to change our current unprofitable situations. Moses had to exercise humility when his father-in-law got in his business. You may know how it is to have your father-in-law involve himself in your business. As a man, you want to be head of your household and handle your own business. You're not trying to have anyone tell you what to do. But, Moses humbled himself and listened to his father-in-law's advice. He was blessed and revived because he changed his structured management and implemented new administrative plans. Gentlemen, sometimes a little humility will take us a long way. If we remember we can benefit from another's wisdom and experience, we do well.

Another key to receiving mentorship is *looking at the bigger picture*. Moses receiving Jethro's mentorship was not "just about him." We've got to remember Moses didn't just pastor a handful of people, but he was in charge of millions. The lives of others were attached to his submission to the advice sent from God through his father-in-law. We have lives attached to us as well. We must keep in mind that there is always a bigger picture which involves other people.

Accept the mentorship God sends your way, so you can be blessed as well as others. Has God been trying to get you to change your methods and handle things differently? Has God sent someone to you to help you and have you rejected his or her advice? Gentlemen, it could be the reason you are frustrated in your life. If you are experiencing "burnout" this means you can't continue to operate the way you've been operating. You need to make a change. You need a mentor.

COMMUNICATE LIFE SKILLS AND
PRINCIPLES IN YOUR COMMUNITY

I said earlier, a mentor communicates life skills and principles. Our communities desperately need this. Men, not only must we be mentored, we must mentor. We have a responsibility to mentor the young men who are around us. When we look around our communities and churches we should have a "sense of responsibility" for future generations. We should have a burning desire to love and help as many young men as we can. We have a responsibility to give young men the benefit of the wisdom we have. We need to share our experiences and mistakes and let them know we've messed up. We can't be hypocritical and act like we've never done anything wrong. These young men are very discerning and are looking for "realness." We can encourage them not to travel the paths we choose and give them some better options and different alternatives to consider.

We need to be men who mentor and communicate life skills and principles to our boys at the earliest age possible. We don't need to wait until they have chaos and trouble in their lives and then try to reach them. Solid life principles should be instilled in them by the time they are entering high school. They should be able to understand honesty, integrity, character, and have a sense of identity.

You don't have to be spiritual to discern our young men are in trouble in this 21st century. Their problems are far greater than ours were at their age. We can turn the daily news on and see them "dropping off like flies." Our young men are greeted with violence on a daily basis. They are being murdered at school, in front of stores, in their front yards, on the playgrounds, and so forth. The "innocent" are dying as well as the "troubled." Some of our young men are strung out on drugs to numb their daily pain of the misfortunes they face in life. Some become involved in gangs looking for acceptance and security. Some struggle with their sexuality and are trying to figure out who they really are. I believe if men would become involved in mentoring our young men, we could make a difference. Although we can't stop *all* of the violence, drug abuse, gang activities, sexual struggles, etc., we can help to influence a young man to stop unhealthy behaviors or redirect a young boy to never enter into them.

It's important that we begin to instill in our youth an "I can do it" mentality. We can impart into them the skills needed to handle their lives properly, make good decisions, and handle criticism. They need to know how to handle themselves when their peers are pressuring them to do wrong. They need the assurance from us that we are "covering" them, concerned and looking out for them. We shouldn't be putting young people down, dogging them until they feel like *nothing.* First, we should be inspiring them by being good examples. Then, we should be encouraging them by speaking positives into their lives to help them understand that they are *somebody* and have the potential for a bright future. They must know and hear of the greatness which lies within them. And lastly, we should be willing to take a few moments from our busy schedules to spend time with our youth.

IT DOESN'T TAKE MUCH

I have a minister in my congregation who tells me, "just a touch on the shoulder will make a big difference in the lives of people." I agree. Sometimes it is just a pat on the back, a touch on the shoulder, a genuine smile, a nice firm handshake, or a kind word spoken that makes the difference in people's lives. It is the thing we consider to be small and irrelevant that will change a life. It really doesn't take much.

I remember being helped years ago by a man who didn't know I was dealing with self-esteem issues. This man walked up to me, laid his hand on my shoulder and said, "You know...I see something in you. Anything you want to accomplish in life...*you can do it!*" Do you know this made a significant difference in my life? Just those few words, "Anything you want to accomplish in life...you can do it!" I never forgot it. I can still see the man's face now. He spoke those few words with sincerity and walked away. Those words always give me encouragement especially during difficult times.

I want to impel you as men, today, to pick up your mantle of responsibility. I want you to understand the urgency of our call to be the voice of reason in a perplexing society. We are called to be the voice of constancy in a world of confusion. Wavering up and down and fighting over who is politically right or wrong is not the answer. You and I, the men of God, are called to become involved and concerned in this earthly realm today for our young men. It is part of my assignment as well as yours. Brothers, we have to wake up from our slumber and get to work. After all, there is a cry for help from our young men, and you, as a man, need to mentor.

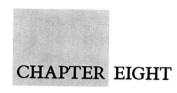

CHAPTER EIGHT

Twelve Life-Changing Principles for Men
Part I

There are twelve life changing principles every man should know and practice. Not only should he know and practice them, he should instill and teach them to his son and his son's sons. I believe single mothers would greatly benefit by implanting them in their son's life to create a legacy where they become the men God intends for them to be. These *life changing principles* won't work if you just read about them. Reading is only the first step. In order to see their effectiveness in your life, application must be applied. If you commit to these practical steps you will experience wonderful victories in every aspect of your life.

PRINCIPLE NUMBER 1
LEARN TO WIN THE BATTLE IN YOUR HEAD
(THOUGHT LIFE)
(Psalm 101:2-3, Romans 12:2)

A man's mind can be likened to a powerful magnet that attracts whatever he assigns it, or a giant sponge that absorbs everything he comes in contact with. His mind is a powerful tool which can either work "for him" or "against him" depending upon how he chooses to use it. Therefore, a man's thoughts are very important and *every one* counts for something, whether good or bad. Everything a man has ever done or will ever do originates in his mind first—*in his thought life.* Most men don't even realize they are only "one thought" away from *success* or failure, breakthrough or breakdown, prosperity or poverty, friend or foe. So, what a man constantly thinks and meditates on will always dictate his outcome.

This is where the war for your mind begins. Your mind is a battlefield and everyday you face an ongoing battle inside of your head. You are under attack each day by the enemy. The enemy plans his assaults against you to try to hinder or control you. He understands the principle that if he can control your mind, he can control you. Since he possesses the knowledge of how powerful your mind is, he tries to find ways to load you with negative information with the intention to turn your focus away from God. His job has been made easier in the 21st century because of all the new and unending advancements of technology which have infiltrated most homes today. He is ruthless and uses whatever is in your path: iPod, television, radio, internet, video cams or anything else to influence your thought life to *his destructive will.* He wants your mind and will stop at nothing to get it.

A man can win this battle and learn to control his thought life in two ways. First, by continually renewing his mind with the Word of God, which says, *"...be not conformed to this world* (society's way of thinking), *but be ye transformed by the renewing of your mind..."* (Romans 12:2, Bishop Francisco version). Second, by making a conscious decision to be careful and monitor what he sets in front of his eyes. Psalm 101:2-3 says, *"I will behave myself wisely in a perfect way...I will walk within my house with a perfect heart. I will set no wicked thing before mine eyes..."*

You have a choice in the matter. You control your thought life by what or who you allow to influence you: the enemy, society, others or God. God designed your mind to reproduce whatever you put in it and gave you total control. So, whatever is in front of you on a consistent basis or whatever you look at is what you are going to reproduce in life. If you allow yourself to be full of the negative and unhealthy influences the enemy sets before you, you will reproduce those negative, defeating images. For instance, if you are consumed with watching Jerry Springer and Maury shows, your life will more than likely be filled with drama. If you are consumed with MTV and videos where women are dancing and leaving little to your imagination, you will more than likely have a lot of "lust" issues. If you are consumed with playing violent video games, you may be one step away from exploding. *Remember, you have the ability to reproduce what is in front of you.* You don't want to reproduce such things as: lust, greed, anger, unhealthy addictions and so forth. You can't win the battle in your thought life being consumed with all that negativity.

On the other hand, you have an opportunity to reproduce great things if God's Word and vision for your life is in front of you. You will see yourself as God sees you and visualize what God has for you. The Word of God will enable you to see success, prosperity, good health, great opportunities, and the abundance of blessings all around you. If you saturate yourself with the light of God's Word, you will be able to reproduce the victorious, successful plans He has for you.

Everyday God tries to turn your attention towards Him. The Lord is trying to get in your head. He wants first priority in your thought life. He wants to be the first and last person you think about everyday. Invite God to help you transform your thought life. Study God's Word, learn His principles and apply them to your life so you can lead a productive life.

The Word of God can help you to release old thinking, paradigms and knowledge that have been etched in your psyche. As you renew your mind, it will help you to rethink your current life strategy and evaluate what's not working in your life spiritually, financially, physically, and so on. You will be able to replace your old thinking, reprogram yourself and reproduce what God has already planned for you in your future and in the present.

God desires for you to reproduce yourself as He sees you, as a great, mighty, anointed, victorious man of valor. I dare you to use God's Word and paint an image of yourself succeeding, advancing and producing. Take a moment right now to paint a picture on the canvas of your mind of yourself dealing effectively and constructively with life. You will reproduce this picture. Get the victory in your mind, no matter what your circumstances currently look like. See yourself walking in it, living in it, operating in it and doing it because God's Word says so and wait for the manifestation. Take control of your thought life today. You have what it takes to win the battle in your head.

PRINCIPLE NUMBER 2
DEVELOP A LIFE PLAN FOR SUCCESS
AND ACT INTENTIONALLY
(Proverbs 24:3, 4)

In Chapter Five, I shared how the simplicity of success comes from spending time in God's presence and listening to what He has to say about your life. My dear brother, that is not the end. Once you hear what God is saying, then you must plan. *If you fail to plan; you plan to fail!* Proverbs 24:3-4 TLB says, "Any enterprise is built by wise planning, becomes strong through common sense, and profits wonderfully by keeping abreast of the facts." Your life can be changed for an eternity if you incorporate wise planning, common sense and keep abreast of the facts. However, you cannot pick and choose; all three need to be incorporated in order to maintain a healthy balance in your lifestyle. If you feel you have good common sense, but don't ever plan or keep abreast of the facts, you may not ever see your desired results. If you become a wise planner, utilize common sense and keep abreast of the facts, you will produce positive results and experience the blessings of God.

a. Set some goals in life. Map out your life plan. Map out what you are called to do. Write it down. Put it in front of you and begin to set it in motion. Get an understanding of God's assignment and know where He wants to take you to. Men who don't plan or set goals shoot for whatever comes along their path. You could say they operate haphazardly—meaning: Whatever happens, happens! Nonetheless, you've got to set some intentional goals in your life.

As a man you have to operate intentionally. You have to have an idea of where you are going. If you are married and want peace in your household, don't ever give your wife the impression you don't know what's going on. Always know where you're going. *Please don't ever say, "I don't know!" or ask, "What do you want to do?" Wrong answer!* You are the one God set as a covering for your home and your future. Even if you are not married, understand there must be some goals set in place in your life. You don't want to walk aimlessly about trying to figure out what life is all about without knowing where you are going. You want to set some goals, make them clear, and measurable. Don't set goals that are impossible, go for something you can make happen. Be realistic!

b. Make a commitment to constantly evaluate the goals you set. Once you set a goal or determine to do something then evaluate where you are. I have always been goal-oriented and goal-driven. I have always sat down and written out my goals. To this day, I can go back fifteen years and look at the five, ten, fifteen and twenty year plans that I made. I always revisit my plans to make sure I am on track. Did I accomplish everything I planned? No! But, I still had some goals set in place and had an idea of where I was going.

I currently have a five, ten, and twenty year plan which I look at often. I have become accustomed to evaluating my plans because I'm fully aware they will never materialize if I don't. They will be forgotten. So, make sure your plan is in place, constantly inspect and evaluate the goals you set.

c. Turn your good intentions into actions. Many men come up with great ideas but never implement them. Make sure you take your good intentions and put them into action. You don't have to have a thousand ideas, just one good one. Just operate and perform according to the goals specified in your plan.

Remember, people check you out all the time. There is always somebody watching your life and making an assessment of the type of person you are. When you don't follow-through on your good intentions, others may see you as a quitter or just a talker. This affects your relationships in a negative way whether it is with your wife, children, friend, co-workers, supervisor, etc. You don't want to be known as a man with a "lot of fluff" or the one who talks a good talk but can't walk the walk. You want to make sure you turn your good intentions into action. If you say you're going to do something, then do it. Don't say it, if you are not going to do it. If you can't make something happen, don't say you will.

If you make a mistake, just admit you messed up. There have been plenty of times I said I was going to make things happen and didn't. I just went back and said, "I messed up! I didn't make it happen, but I have another plan." This gave me a chance to redeem myself and turn my good intentions into actions.

Acting intentionally means accepting responsibility for the goals and visions we have set in place. That's all it means. Men who are acting intentionally, are saying, I'm taking responsibility for the goals and visions I've set in place and I'm going to make sure they are carried out. We must develop a life plan for success and act intentionally.

PRINCIPLE NUMBER 3
MEN NEED WORK
(Genesis 2:2, 4, 15; 2 Thessalonians 3:11-13, MSG)

"God took the Man and set him down in the Garden of Eden to work the ground and keep it in order" (Genesis 2:15 MSG). Men were created to work. It is part of our inner strength. Throughout this book, I have shown you how the enemy studies the male and knows what buttons to push. A "man's work" is another one of those buttons. I believe the enemy will attack a man's work ethic in two extremes: First, he will cause a man to become a workaholic. This man will become so obsessed with his work to the point where he doesn't spend time with his family, his church, or even his relationship with God. He just feels an impulsive urge to work, work, work!

He allows himself to become so consumed with his career until it becomes his whole purpose in life. The enemy gets him off track and confuses him about his priorities which causes his important relationships to suffer.

Second, if the enemy doesn't get a man to become a workaholic then he drives him to the other extreme of not working at all. This man will either spiritualize it by sitting around doing nothing, saying, "I am waiting on the Lord...God is going to move on my behalf...The Lord told me to just hold out." Or he will find a woman or someone else to take care of him.

We have a generation of men in today's time who are looking for "mommas." So, rather than knowing how to provide and care for themselves and their families, they look for someone else to do it. This is why so many men will sit on their rusty behinds and allow their wives to take care of them. Yes, I'm going to say it just like that. It is an abomination in the sight of God. I know it's raw, but if you are that man, I want to shake you out of your place of comfort.

The apostle Paul told the Thessalonians, *"Don't you remember the rule we had when we lived with you? 'If you don't work, you don't eat.'" And now we're getting reports that a bunch of lazy good-for-nothings are taking advantage of you. This must not be tolerated. We command them to get to work immediately—no excuses, no arguments—and earn their own keep. Friends, don't slack off in doing your duty"* (2 Thessalonians 3:11-13 MSG). The same rule should still apply today. Even though your wife is capable, she is not going to be held accountable for what God has purposed for you to do—WORK! God's plan and purpose is for us to recognize the divine order He orchestrated for mankind and function in it.

The Lord doesn't want us on either end of the contention. God wants us right in the middle. He wants us to balance our work and our leisure time, whereby we can be a blessing. God was the first and ultimate example of how a man should balance his work and leisure time. *"Thus the heavens and the earth were finished, and all the host of them. And on the seventh day God ended his work which he had made; and he rested on the seventh day from all his work which he had made. And God blessed the seventh day, and sanctified it: because that in it he had rested from all his work which God created and made"* (Genesis 2:2-4). God worked and He rested. Now, that is called, BALANCE!

Once a man gets in the GAP or spends time in his cave, God will teach him how to bring balance into his life. He can balance his workload and everything else God has called him to do. You don't have to fall into the area of being a workaholic or not desiring to work at all. You can find the true balance which only comes from the unction of the Holy Spirit.

God not only wants you to work, He desires for every man to become skilled at what he does. In this 21st century there are so many opportunities for men to advance in their various fields. There are many ways to educate yourself or to acquire an education for a degree or a certified program. You can become an expert in whatever field you choose. Education adds value to your life—meaning: It can take your worth from minimum wage to a six figure income.

Also, I encourage you to enjoy the work you do. Find a job in something of interest. If you don't find it right away, it doesn't mean don't work at all. Do something until you get to where you want to be. Working does more things for you as a man than you will ever know. Remember, men were meant to work.

PRINCIPLE NUMBER 4
NEVER BE SATISFIED WITH ANYTHING
LESS THAN GOD'S BEST
(Zephaniah 1:12-13)

Some learn to live with second best and accept their present status. I am challenging men to recognize God desires something better than second class living. Sometimes we fall into a rut of accepting second best and become content. *You have to learn how to not be satisfied.* If something knocks you down, you have to learn how to get back up. Don't just accept it and say, "...that's just the way it is!" Even if a doctor gives you a death sentence, don't just accept it. Get the Word of God and declare, "I shall not die, but live!" Why? Because the Word of God says what *His* best is for you. If financial ruin comes as a forecast, don't accept it! Declare, "I shall not fail, I will prosper." Learn how to refuse the devil's report and accept God's report for your life.

I want you to get a vision of upgrading your lifestyle in your mind right now. It's difficult for us sometimes because we are so comfortable and content. Did you know "contentment" breeds mediocrity and mediocrity breeds a slow destruction? It's true! When you rest in contentment and complacency you will find yourself overcome by destruction. Contentment always breeds weeds. I will give you a good example:

> Several years ago I had a moment of nostalgia concerning my father's garden. After my moment, I came to the conclusion that I wanted a garden in my backyard. I decided I wanted fresh watermelon and cantaloupe. I made up my mind not to buy any from the

grocery store because I was determined to grow and eat my very own.

So, I went to work and tilled the dirt and planted my seeds. For the first month, the garden was impeccable. I was so proud when the little watermelon and cantaloupe plants started shooting up out of the ground. I was proud because it was immaculate and everything was in place, but mediocrity gradually set in when the weather started getting hotter!

Two months later... I looked at my garden, I couldn't tell whether it was watermelon, cantaloupe or grass. I had gotten started, but gradually allowed contentment to overtake me, and contentment allowed the weeds to overtake my garden.

This is what happens when you become content and don't attend to what God has assigned you. The weeds in your life will overtake you and nobody will know if you are a child of God or not, because they won't be able to distinguish you from all the other mess in your life. So, it's important that we not allow contentment, defeat and second best to settle in—no matter how hot or difficult it gets.

As men, we are required by God to always lift the bar. Zephaniah 1:12-13 says, *"And it shall come to pass at that time, that I will search Jerusalem with candles, and punish the men that are settled on their lees: that say in their heart, The LORD will not do good, neither will he do evil. Therefore their goods shall become a booty, and their houses a desolation: they shall also build houses, but not inhabit them;*

and they shall plant vineyards, but not drink the wine thereof." This scripture refers to men who are stuck in mediocrity; Men who say in their heart, "God isn't going to move one way or another, so I might as well be satisfied the way I am and stay right here." No! You have to bring it up to another level. I believe God was saying to the Israelite men, "If you don't take responsibility and bring it up to another level, then I can't let you enjoy what you are laboring for," meaning: If you don't upgrade your mentality or your lifestyle or your spirituality or your methodology, then someone else will enjoy the profit of your labor because you are satisfied.

Mediocrity is another one of the things the enemy uses against men. We must resist it with all of our strength. We can't afford to be couch potatoes! We cannot become settled, satisfied, and content in our lives and feel like "if it's not broken, why fix it or improve upon it." We have to take care of ourselves, so we can have longevity—spiritually, physically, materially, socially, financially, mentally and in every respect. We can do this by never settling for less than God's best.

PRINCIPLE NUMBER 5
GIVE GOD 10% OF ALL YOUR INCREASE,
SAVE 10% AND LIVE OFF OF 80%
(Proverbs 13:11)

We have to learn how to be good stewards over our finances. I believe it is helpful when we remember this: *100% of our money belongs to God.* God allows us to keep 90% and we only give 10% back to God. Some brothers have a "here we go again" mentality whenever money or giving is mentioned. If you have this type of mentality, I encourage you to change it today. You can't receive what God has for you by being tight with Him. You can be tight with whoever else you want to, but I plead with you, *don't be tight with God.* You will never be blessed living this way.

Deuteronomy 8:18 says, *"But thou shalt remember the Lord thy God that gives you the power to get wealth."* If you forget God, God will forget you. You have to learn how to be a tither, saver, and investor. *GIVE God 10% of all your increase, SAVE 10%, and LIVE off of 80%.* It's the *10-10-80 principle* which enables us to give, save and live.

We need to be living examples of this principle to our children. In fact, we must teach our children to give God 10%, save 10% and wisely live off of 80%. I have taught and still teach my children this principle. I started by giving them an allowance when they were young. This may seem like a small gesture, but I was establishing lifetime habits in them. I also taught them the importance of using their 80% for substance, such as land and finances in the bank, rather than spending it all on "stuff" which has no value.

To my young brothers who are spending all their money on 22" rims (or "22's") and expensive sound systems for their cars—STOP! It may look impressive to others, but how much money do you have in the bank? What do you own that isn't depreciating? How much are you worth? Those who matter in society today are those who bring something to the table. Don't get caught up in feeling like you have to measure up with everybody else. The time will come, if you enact the principles I am sharing with you, that ten years from now you'll be financially stable while others are in debt from trying to live up to the expectations of others.

Banks do not measure your success by the gold chains, luxury cars, designer clothes, or diamond rings you possess. While others may be impressed by you driving a $50,000 car and wearing a $1,000 suit and $2,000 worth of jewelry, it does not impress a banker. When you go to the bank to make a major purchase or conduct business, you may go in looking like a million dollars, but their concern is your portfolio. I don't want to be the bearer of bad news, but they don't care about your "bling-bling." I am encouraging you, rather than trying to look like a million—*work at securing a million!* The first thing the bank will ask you is, "What do you own? What kind of collateral do you have?" Gentleman, "bling-bling" can't be your answer. It doesn't matter to them if you have the best car, wardrobe and "bling" in town!

Many years ago when my wife and I were first married, I had a solid gold ring. When we were having financial difficulties and desperately needed money I decided to pawn my gold ring. I took my ring to the pawn shop thinking I had something valuable because it was solid gold. The man looked at my ring and said, "I might be able to give you $75.00." I was shocked. Did he say, "$75.00?" That was nothing! I wanted to smack the man because I needed some money plus the ring was solid gold. What I'm saying to you is, "the stuff" we think are assets, are not! When you want to build a portfolio, they want to know about houses, land, stocks and bonds, mutual funds, money markets and whatever else you have of value. Society rates you based on the value that you possess.

The time has come for us to take the blinders off. It's my responsibility as a man of God to push men to make sure they aren't just perpetrating. I'm not interested in men who just want to give grand appearances. I want to push *real men* who are serious about their economic wealth and relevance in today's society; men who can be a resource to someone else and help other men get where they need to be.

If you need help managing the 90% of finances which has been entrusted to you, talk to someone you know is financially stable. Seek out financial counseling and talk to someone who can teach you how to be a good steward. It's going to require a word that many don't like to hear—sacrifice! It may require you to stop compulsive spending, excessive dining out, wearing expensive suits and shoes and wearing your fine jewelry. You will be alright! Eventually, it will pay off and not only will you be blessed, you'll be able to bless the lives of others.

Many times people look at where you are *now* with no consideration of where you have been. They look at me and my family and just see "BLESSED." I have taken my wife through bankruptcy and lost everything we owned. We know what it is to be broken down to the grass root. We know what it's like to have your belongings and car repossessed. I don't want anyone to get the impression that my family and I have never been through anything. We have been through a whole lot. We learned the hard way that we had to get in the "God-appointed place," stop trying to impress others, and operate using God's financial principles. Because of this, my family and I have become recipients of the blessings of God. We've learned to honor God and have been honoring God with the tithe and above for so many years that whatever need we may have God automatically releases it into our lives. Therefore, we are blessed *today* because of our faithfulness to operate in His financial principles.

God is not a respecter of persons. If He can do it for me and my family, He will do it for you. The only stipulation is, you must be willing to operate in God's financial principles long-term. Don't think of these principles as short-term where you commit this week while all is well and you are feeling good. Be consistent. God is not a yo-yo! Make a commitment to follow the principles I have shared and allow God to bless your finances.

PRINCIPLE NUMBER 6
YOUR FIRST MAJOR PURCHASE SHOULD BE LAND
AND NOT AN AUTOMOBILE
(Jeremiah 29:4-6)

George Foreman made a statement one day which I wrote down because I thought it was worth sharing. He said, "It embarrasses me to think of all those years I was buying silk suits and alligator shoes that were hurting my feet and cars that I parked and dust would build up on them." His statement made me want to instill in men even more to learn to purchase things of value. Your first major purchase should be land. You may start with a small lot, but own some dirt somewhere. Even if you have to drive a "hoopty," *own some land!*

I shared with the men in my congregation a couple of years ago, "I don't necessarily have to pastor a church where everybody is driving a Lexus or Mercedes and looking good, but don't have anything. You don't have to showboat for me or anyone else." I would be thrilled to know they owned some land and drove a "hoopty" rather than see them driving a shiny Cadillac and have no type of net worth.

I know we need transportation to tend to our business and care for our families. I'm not saying you don't need a car. You just might not need a fancy BMW right now. Your car is going to depreciate as soon as you drive it off the lot. It's going to be worth thousands of dollars less. If you drove it off the lot and decided to turn around and ask for a refund, the car dealership would not give you what you *just paid* for it. It would be considered a used car and would not be worth what you paid for it just five minutes ago. An automobile is a depreciating asset which automatically decreases in value while land is an appreciating asset which automatically increases in value. Why not purchase land which increases its value? If you don't have any land, you need to work on it!

This may seem tough to some because most of us live for the moment. However, I endeavor to teach young men to be blessed long-term. You can't be a *real man* until you own some land. Genesis 2:7 says, *"...God formed man out of the dust of the earth..."* Don't you think you ought to own some of what you are created out of? You should have authority and dominion and own some of what you were created out of.

I can't say it enough—most things we pursue in life have little value. I endeavor to challenge you and give you something to think about beginning with this: The bank will loan you $40,000 to buy a Lexus you can't afford; however, if you wanted the same $40,000 to purchase a condo or a townhouse, you would be told you don't qualify. Why do I say this? The enemy doesn't want you to have any value. First Peter 5:8 warns us, *"Be sober, be vigilant; because your adversary the devil, as a roaring lion, walketh about, seeking whom he may devour."* The enemy will always set you up for failure. He will have you spend *all* your money on "worthless stuff." This definitely is not God's will for your life. God wants you to have something that's "real and valuable."

Here is God's mandate to men in Jeremiah 29:4-6: *"Thus saith the LORD of hosts, the God of Israel, unto all that are carried away captives, whom I have caused to be carried away from Jerusalem unto Babylon; Build ye houses, and dwell in them; and plant gardens, and eat the fruit of them; Take ye wives, and beget sons and daughters; and take wives for your sons, and give your daughters to husbands, that they may bear sons and daughters; that ye may be increased there, and not diminished..."* God set the priorities for men in verses 5-6. The first thing God wanted man to do was build houses. My question to you is, how can a man build a house if he has no land? Houses can't be built on air. So, obtaining land must be a priority in a man's life in order for him to build, dwell, plant, eat and enjoy his wife and children. The last part of the above scripture says, "...*that ye may be increased... and not diminished...*" This is God's will for you. Land will never decrease or diminish you; it will always increase you.

I want to see men whose value and worth are defined and determined by land. History even tells us this is imperative! Do you ever stop to think why nations fight over land? It is the only thing that is real. That's why they call land—*real estate*. It is the only thing that is real. The car you drive is not *real* estate. You may think I am trying to "rain on your parade." I'm not! I'm just encouraging you to add value to your life by purchasing some land because it enacts a principle in your life. Your first major purchase should be land and not an automobile.

CHAPTER NINE

Twelve Life-Changing Principles for Men
Part II

PRINCIPLE NUMBER 7
CHOOSE YOUR SPOUSE BASED ON COMPATIBILITY
AND NOT THE SIZE OF HER BIKINI
(Proverbs 31:30)

Some of you are looking at the wrong thing. Sizes change. A good preacher friend of mine once told me of the advice he gave to a young man considering marriage. He told him, "If you are just marrying her for beauty, you better check some things out first. I want you to go look at her mother because thirty years from now, that's what you are going to have." This wasn't meant to be a derogatory statement. He was just informing the young man of the evolution involved in human life. We have to remember changes *will* occur so you can't marry based on what you see today. Reality says, "it's not going to remain the same." You may have an attractive woman by your side today, but, if she is intellectually challenged, can't communicate, or add to you socially, academically, spiritually, or morally—think again! Young men who get excited over the "hotties" or nice-looking girls in the videos they watch, need to realize, there is more to a woman than being cute and flaunting her voluptuous curves. We live in a society where there are a whole lot of over-developed young ladies with under-developed minds.

They look like women but don't know how to act like women. So, you have to look for a woman who can do more than just dance and look "hot."

Proverbs 31:30 says, *"Favour is deceitful, and beauty is vain: but a woman that feareth the LORD, she shall be praised."* You want to find a virtuous Godly woman. Choose your spouse based on compatibility. Choose your spouse based on your likeness of vision, dreams, and potential. Ask yourself the question: What does she bring to the table? You don't want to choose a person based on outward appearance.

When I first saw my wife, and we captured one another's attention, I saw more than her physical side. She can also bear witness to the fact that I tested her. Yes, I did! I knew where God was taking me. I knew I was going to require someone who could deal with the challenges which lay ahead. I knew it wasn't going to be an easy road, and I needed someone who could help me get to my place of destiny. I didn't need someone I had to pick up and carry the whole way. I needed someone who could help me when I needed help, encourage me when I needed encouragement, support me when I needed support and walk with me as a source of strength. I didn't need a woman who was just going to stand there snapping her fingers asking me, "When are you going to get me my new sofa?"

Compatibility is a plus to any man's life. The Bible says, *"Be ye not unequally yoked together with unbelievers..."* (2 Corinthians 6:14). This means you have a responsibility, whether male or female, to connect with someone who is spiritually in sync with you. Not only spiritually, but you should be compatible in terms of academics, social skills, finances, value systems, etc. It's very difficult if you hook up with a person who is a recluse and you are a social activist. While you enjoy being in the public socializing, your spouse may love staying in the comfort of her home. You may marry a woman who likes to party every night while you are focused on more important things in life. You may have aspirations of a 4,000 square foot house, and your spouse may be satisfied living in a one bedroom apartment with two cribs in the bedroom. You may have dreams and visions and all your spouse wants to know is, "What's wrong with where we are?"

A word of caution for young men: You are a prime target for the enemy. He has young ladies (some refer to them as "hoochies") out here looking for you because they see increase on you. They see a college graduate in the making, a future entrepreneur, banker, producer, architect, doctor or lawyer. If they can't get you now, they will keep trying. Even if it means having your baby with no hopes of marriage in sight. Some are just satisfied owning some of you and knowing they have their claws in you for the next twenty years. They know every time you get a raise or a promotion they get one. Please understand, I'm not trying to speak in a derogatory manner about women. However, I am encouraging you to think, think, think! Think compatibility, think destiny, but do not think bikini size!

PRINCIPLE NUMBER 8
DWELL WITH YOUR WIFE ACCORDING TO KNOWLEDGE
(1 Peter 3:7)

" *...ye husbands, dwell with them according to knowledge, giving honour unto the wife, as unto the weaker vessel, and as being heirs together of the grace of life; that your prayers be not hindered*" (1 Peter 3:7). Many married men do not realize the significance of this principle, yet it affects the most important area of their life—their prayer life. Some know this principle but for some reason they choose to ignore or overlook it as if it doesn't apply to them. They just want to forget it's written in the Bible. Many husbands are praying today, some are even fasting, but are receiving few results. They are sincerely longing for God to use them, but He can't and won't until they honor and dwell with their wives according to knowledge. From experience I want to persuade men to never overlook or forget this principle again because you hinder your own progress.

I recognized years ago, what I accomplish in life is directly linked to how I treat my wife. When my ministry was stifled, I asked God, "What's going on? Why is the ministry not flourishing? I am working and doing everything I am supposed to do." God had me examine myself. He showed me my ministry's suffering was in direct correlation to how I was treating my wife. He showed me my first church, which is my ministry to my wife, was messed up. This was the reason why my prayers and my ministry were hindered. You may wonder sometimes, why aren't my prayers being answered? Why does it seem my prayers go no further than the ceiling? My answer: *Check out how you have been treating your wife.* Many marriage relationships aren't where they should be because husbands are looking at their wives as the problem when they should be looking at themselves. They are not treating their wives as equals or heirs. Some husbands are trying to accomplish great and noble things while stepping all over their wives. Then you have other husbands who are simply abrasive to their wives for no reason. God did not place a woman in your life for you to abuse her—verbally or physically. God desires for you to dwell with her according to knowledge and honor her as the weaker vessel. Your wife being a weaker vessel does not mean she doesn't exhibit strength and tenacity. Although they have the ability to make powerful things happen, we must remember, on the inside, they are fragile and delicate vessels. The way we treat and respond to them matters in God's sight. So, until you honor your wife, consider your prayers hindered and going no higher than the ceiling. Those things you are believing God for aren't happening because you haven't come into knowledge of your wife. You haven't begun to honor her yet.

"...Dwell with them according to knowledge," means being knowledgeable about the woman God has placed in your life. We honor our wives when we study them and know what makes them tick. It means a lot to a woman when her husband knows what motivates and moves her. It excites her to know her man has studied her enough to know when she is happy or sad. When you understand her uniqueness which sets her apart from other women, she notices. When you take on the responsibility and mandate God has given you to know her, *your relationship will flourish.* Yes, gentlemen, we must know our women. This is an honorable thing in the sight of God and your wife.

Often we learn our wives through trial and error. For instance, if February 14th comes and you didn't give your wife any flowers and she says, "Jill got flowers and LaQuita got some candy today at work," she is giving you a hint. Instead of you wanting to know what's for dinner, you need to know you've made a big mistake. Next, you need to admit your mistake and learn from it. When February 14th comes around next year, you've dealt with your wife according to knowledge and you know on that day she needs to have flowers or candy or both. You may not understand the rationale behind your wife, but at least you know what moves her. She needs to know you cared and thought enough about her to produce what moves her. I guarantee when you do this, you will experience another level in your relationship.

I could send my wife a dozen roses, however, it doesn't move her. Although most ladies love flowers, my wife is not one of them. My mother loves flowers. Husbands usually have problems in this area. We think because our mothers loved certain things, our wives will as well. This couldn't be further from the truth. Before getting married I always bought my mother flowers so my first instinct was to buy my wife some. I would buy them, and although she appreciated them gingerly, I began to discern in my spirit, flowers didn't move her. So, now I dwell not in ignorance, but according to knowledge. Rather than spending sixty dollars on a dozen roses, I spend the money to purchase something she really desires. What roses do for your wife, a day at the spa will do for mine! Therefore, I have learned how to dwell with my wife according to knowledge and know how to minister to her.

Husbands, you can't walk in ignorance for twenty years. If you've been married five or ten years and you're still asking, "What do you like?" or "What's wrong with you?" it's time for the light switch to come on. Somewhere along the line you've got to wake up and know what time it is. You've got to dwell with, you've got to learn, you've got to study, and you've got to know your wife. Operate in this principle and see if you don't begin receiving answers to your prayers. Those things you have been striving to do for so long should begin to manifest as you treat your wife with honor, understanding and delight. God will honor you for honoring the woman He has put in your life. Remember, **Knowledge + Honor = Answered Prayer.**

PRINCIPLE NUMBER 9
'FESS UP, IF YOU MESS UP
(Proverbs 23:13)

"He that covereth his sins shall not prosper: but whoso

---

confesseth and forsaketh them shall have mercy" (Proverbs 23:13). This is a hard area for men because of a stronghold called *pride*. We can be so full of pride when it comes to acknowledging our faults or admitting we made a mistake. We seem to revert back to the nature of our father, Adam, who was the king of blame. Adam didn't run to confess his "mess-up." He ran and hid. He tried to cover up his sin. When He was confronted by God, he immediately blamed the woman in his life (Genesis 3:8-12). If we are truthful with ourselves, we have the tendency to do the same thing.

In order to move forward in the things of God, and not cut off our blessings, we must acknowledge when we are wrong. This attitude of not being able to acknowledge wrong in our lives builds barriers and cuts us off from God's divine supply in our life. Also, it builds barriers with others. When you don't 'fess up to the wrong in your life, you bring offense to people by not acknowledging your mistakes. You can cut key people out of your life who were assigned to be a blessing to you. We have to remind ourselves what is more important and 'fess up if we are wrong. We need those key relationships more than we need that spirit of pride hanging around. Admit your mistakes, forsake your ways and accept the mercy. We sow seeds of increase when we admit our wrong, but seeds of destruction, if we don't.

I made a commitment to myself to walk in integrity and speak the truth at all times. If I make a mistake before my wife, I've discovered it's better to say, "Honey, I messed up...I don't have an excuse...I don't have a reason...I just made a mistake and I need to move forward!" It's better to do this than try to create a story.

Integrity for men is of the utmost importance. Men have an inclination to function more using their short-term memory

158

while women utilize their long- term memory. In case you haven't noticed, *women remember everything you say!* For example, you may have had a conversation on a Thursday afternoon in 1980 while sitting on the tan sofa. Do you remember this conversation and details? Probably not, but your woman does! With all probability, you can't even remember what you said last week, not to mention years ago. Sometimes we just forget what we said. This is why it's important to always be genuine and truthful in your communications.

Trying to prove a point and constantly covering up past tracks is foolish. You will never see prosperity or God's favor and blessings. Do the right thing. 'Fess up, if you mess up. I know the temptation to cover up your mistake may be present, but do not yield to it. Never allow your personal pride to keep increase from your life. Come clean as fast as you can and keep in mind, *"... whoso confesseth and forsaketh them shall have mercy."*

PRINCIPLE NUMBER 10
YOU MUST NETWORK WITH OTHER PEOPLE
(Ecclesiastes 4:9-10)

There is a popular gospel song entitled *As Long As I Got King Jesus* which seems to really move people. While this song has a very energizing, upbeat tempo and makes a good hand clapping song, it sends a wrong message—*"But long as I got King Jesus...I don't need nobody else."* Occasionally, we may *feel* this way, but contrary to popular belief, *we need other people.* Ecclesiastes 4:9-10 says, *"Two are better than one; because they have a good reward for their labour. For if they fall, the one will lift up his fellow: but woe to him that is alone when he falleth; for he hath not another to help him up."*

Most men feel very confident about their knowledge. I said previously, most men think they know it all, can do it all and have the answer to all. This may catch you by surprise, but I am going to say it anyway—*you don't know everything!* You may think you do, but you don't. None of us do. For instance, a man can dive into the middle of a conversation where he doesn't know anything about finances, but he'll be the first to advise everyone on how to handle theirs. Needless to say, this man's credit may be so messed up that the creditors have to call him on a daily basis to try to get their money. By the end of the conversation, everyone knows this man is financially illiterate. Or, we have the man who is always advising someone on their marriage, and he can't even keep a girlfriend. Go ahead and admit that you don't know it all! You will move farther along in your life.

We have to learn the importance of networking with one another; it is crucial to our growth as men. The *many* roles we have require us to develop and maintain good support systems. Networking and allowing others to become involved and assist you with your assignments in life is not a sign of weakness. Jesus was one of the world's greatest networkers. He networked with fishermen, tax collectors, politicians, women, and so on. He developed healthy relationships and utilized the assistance of others to accomplish His mission on this earth. If networking was important in Jesus' lifetime, it should be in ours as well.

The mentality of "I got it" no longer works in today's times. *What God has assigned you to do requires the assistance of other people.* If you are honest with yourself, you may admit there is some difficulty in this arena. However, you must be willing to learn from others what you don't know. You must be willing to give others permission and access into your life. You must be willing to take a chance. Risk is inevitable in networking because it involves building relationships.

We have to learn how to become vulnerable to another brother and say, "Listen man, I don't know a whole lot about this situation; can you help me out in this area?" I've conveyed this message throughout this book that the greatest problem we have as men, many times, is our pride. Our pride won't allow us to go to another man or a person. Our pride won't allow us to say, "Listen, I want to do this, but I need some help." A wise man will recognize his areas of weakness and then find strong people to under-gird those areas where he is weak.

Networking is simply utilizing the gifts around you. One of the reasons I feel God has blessed my ministry is because I am acquainted with *my strengths* and *my weaknesses*. I'm not too proud to ask for assistance from someone who is proficient in my weak areas. I'm not ashamed to admit I need help in the areas I don't perform well in. I've learned to network with people who can help me in my areas of weakness.

When it comes to intrinsic ministerial things, I let a person who loves it, handle it. I receive tremendous visions with a lot of good plans, however, implementation is not my forte. Once I get a vision, I gently place it in the lap of my wife or others who have the gift of administration and implementation. I network with people who can come up with a plan from my visions. They are the ones who help me bring it all together and make it happen. As they operate in their gifts and I see things unfolding, I can operate in my gift which is to "tweak." I can see when we need to do more of this or less of that. The end result is always amazing when I see the manifestation of my vision come to pass from networking with other people.

Never forget, no man gets anywhere in life solely on his own, so why not learn the art of networking? Here are some do's and don'ts for networking. *Do reach out of your comfort zone.* You've got to network with individuals who can help you. *Don't be too proud.* Pride will sink your ship. God places resources in your reach, but He might not put them in your hand. He may put them in the hands of people around you and you've got to be willing to reach out to receive your needed resources. *Do be open to new ideas and methods of doing things.* God has so much in store for you, but it may not come or look the way you feel it should. Being receptive can open the door for some wonderful opportunities to transpire in your life.

Do share. If you know God has blessed you to be a resourceful person, don't be stingy or snobbish with your expertise. *Do be approachable.* If you know someone needs help, by all means *help them.* If you don't have the resources and know someone who does—allocate. *Today* you may not need the help but there will always be a *tomorrow* where you may. Network with your brothers and be a blessing to one another. *Do operate in confidentiality,* and *don't broadcast* your brother's private business. Make a conscious decision to *be trustworthy.*

You've got to network with other people.

PRINCIPLE NUMBER 11
NEVER EVER LET THE FEAR OF PEOPLE OR CRITICISM HINDER OR STOP YOU
(Proverbs 29:25)

Never ever let the fear of people or criticism hinder or stop you from achieving your dreams in life. Proverbs 29:25 says,

"The fear of man bringeth a snare: but whoso putteth his trust in the LORD shall be safe." The "fear of man" has ensnared many for centuries, and it is no different in the 21st century. Men have died and are dying with their dreams being unfulfilled. They have died with greatness in them that the world has never seen because of this fear. Some had beautiful voices, but the world never heard their songs. Some had designs for magnificent edifices, but they were never built. Some may have had the gift of articulation and were dynamic speakers, but their speeches were never heard. Some may have had answers to political dilemmas, but their solution was never given. Some had the potential to be great authors, but their books were never written. The "fear of people" made them afraid they would make a mess, fail, be laughed at, or rejected. They fell into the trap and couldn't get out. You are still on this earth and have the ability to use your greatness for God and make a difference. Will you?

Some men actually feel their call in life is to make everybody happy. *It's not!* No matter how hard you try or how sincere you are, you will never satisfy everybody. So, your aim in life should be to please God. You should evaluate everything you do by asking the Lord is He pleased. If you are consumed with pleasing people more than God, "the fear of people" has you ensnared. You cannot let the fear of people hinder you from pursuing your destiny. It is a major mistake, especially for men, because our egos tell us we don't want to be embarrassed. So instead of taking a chance and risking embarrassment or letting others get the wrong impression of us, we just stand back and become a chameleon and blend in. God has not called any of us to just blend in. We are called to be different and make an impact in life.

I encourage you to answer the following series of questions very thoughtfully and honestly:

Why do you do what you do? Why do you carry yourself the way you carry yourself? Why do you act the way you act? Why do you say the things you say? Do you do what you do because you think other people want you to do it, or do you do what you do because you believe it's what God assigned you to do? Are you really in your desired profession because it's where God placed you, or did you choose based upon everyone else's opinions? Do you really love people and reach out to them because it's God's assignment, or are you afraid someone may talk about you? Why do you do what you do?

The greater question is this: Who is the "Simon" in your life? As children, we've all played the "Simon says" game. I believe there is a "Simon" in everybody's life. I don't know what your Simon's name is, but there is a Simon who says, "Stand up, sit down, stretch your arm, be quiet, laugh, jump, etc." Who's pulling your strings? Who's causing you to do what you do? I want to challenge you to do what you do because it's your assignment from God. Don't fall prey to peer pressure, whether young or old. Have a conviction about what you do. Don't do anything because of other's personal opinions about you. Do it because you know God has assigned you to do it.

Have you ever seen a man afraid to go home because he fears what the "boys" will think of him? An example of this would be when a group of men get together to play their weekly basketball game. Brother, go home to your wife and children, if you know it's where you should be at the time. Don't be afraid of what the others are going to say. You may hear, "Ah, man you're just 'hen pecked' letting that woman control you like that...man, I don't let my "ole lady" tell me what to do, I handle my business...you've got to know how to handle your business...that's what's wrong with you." No! Don't be a puppet on a string. Don't let the "Simons" cause you to neglect your wife and children. Don't listen to "Simon" telling you to dribble the basketball, hang out with the fellows, and drink beer. Go home because you love your family and you know it's where you belong. Don't stay on the basketball court with your forty-year-old self trying to dunk the ball and do 360's when you should be home.

I ask again: *Why do you do what you do?* Is it because you have a conviction or because you are afraid? If you don't know what God has called and assigned you to do, *find out!* If you don't, you'll continually fall for anything. People will always try to tell you how to handle your business. They will give you "their" assignment and vision for your life, if you receive it. However, people can only control you with your consent. Nothing will change until you decide to take that power out of their hands. When you are not in control you are being controlled. If you can't control your realm of responsibilities (your circumstances, environment, circle of relationships, or God-given assignment) then you are out of control. If this is you today, make a conscious decision, act intentionally and regain control of your life.

The way to stop allowing the fear and opinions of others to control your life is by trusting God. The second half of Proverbs 29:25 says, *"... but whoso putteth his trust in the LORD shall be safe."* Therefore, if you put your trust in God instead of people's opinions, your destiny, family, career, and everything that pertains to you will be safe. *And* the reason it will be safe is because you will be listening and obeying God's voice who knows the plans He has for your life rather than others who think they do. So, my dear brother, pursue your dreams and destiny and never ever let the fear of people or criticism hinder or stop you again in life.

PRINCIPLE NUMBER 12
SURROUND YOURSELF WITH PEOPLE WHO DESIRE MORE THAN THE BARE ESSENTIALS OF LIFE
(Proverbs 13:20)

If you want more out of life then you have to surround yourself with people who desire more out of life. There will always be a group of people who are satisfied with just "getting by." They are genuinely happy right where they are and do not aspire to go any further. You won't go too far being surrounded by this group. You have to get in contact with people who are where you want to be or at least moving in that direction. You cannot associate with people who are satisfied with just getting by because that's what you will become.

Proverbs 13:20 says, *"He that walketh with wise men shall be wise: but a companion of fools shall be destroyed."* This Scripture literally means association brings on assimilation. It means you can adopt the nature, attitude, characteristics and traits of those you associate with to such a degree until you act like them. This is why it is important to always have people in your life who will challenge you and cause you to become better than what you are. Those who don't increase you will eventually decrease you. If you have people who are not challenging you to become your best, you won't because of the "just enough" mentality with which you are associated.

I challenge you by saying this: "If you really want to know what you look like or what type of person you are, look at your *three closest friends*. If you take a good look at your three closest friends, you will see yourself in a mirror. You will find out who you really are. Listen to your friends and you will hear yourself. Observe their mannerisms, vernacular, movements, and attitudes. You will discover you have developed the same. Look at the way they dress and then look at your closet. Do you see any similarities? You can become so close until you unconsciously exhibit the same types of behaviors. So, if you're not satisfied with where you are, consider the friends with whom you have surrounded yourself. They have a lot to do with where you are in life right now.

I truly believe people become products of their environment and have to work very diligently if they desire to go beyond the level of their environment. You have to seek God and ask, "Is this the pinnacle for me...is this the mountaintop... or do You have more in store for me?" If God has more in store for you then surround yourself with people who will rouse and pull more out of you. Being around people who are at a higher level than yourself is good. These individuals will cause you to go to the next level in your life. They will cause you to increase your vocabulary. They will compel you to look at your study habits. They will provoke you to become more proficient in your service to the Lord and His people. They will help you to grow spiritually and won't allow you to be satisfied with just going to church on Sunday morning. These are the types of individuals you should surround yourself with—the ones who increase you and don't decrease you. So, if you are a person who believes there is more to life, if you desire, require and want more, then you need to surround yourself with people who desire more than the bare essentials.

BASIC LIFE PRINCIPLES

These are basic life principles that I have just shared in these last two chapters. God is calling for men to become strong, to be resourced so they can be resources in the world today. Some men may feel these principles aren't grand enough. However, I want to open men's eyes where they can see the things we consider small and insignificant begin to bring the biggest harvest in their lives. The principle of Luke 16:10 tells us if we are faithful in the least, then we will be faithful in much. If you take these basic principles and apply them to your life, I guarantee you, by the end of the year your life will not be the same.

CHAPTER TEN

Hang On To Your Dreams

As I conclude this book we have entered into a new year which has plagued numerous individuals with uncertainty concerning their future. Therefore, I would be remiss not to address some of the great challenges we are now facing in the 21st century. The buzz word today is "economy" and the big question is: "How do we survive the recession and maintain our sanity and dignity in these tough economic downturns?" I realize that I do not have the answers to the economic crisis we are facing and it would be audacious of me to think that I did. Being true to you and to myself, the thing that I feel I can offer you is hope.

As I shared with you in previous chapters, my life has not always been one of ease and good fortune; actually it has been anything but that. I have lived on this earth for half a century and have seen many ups and downs in my lifetime, but God has been good to me and brought me through many challenges. I am sure each of you could resonate with a testimony like that, and you are the ones who I want to encourage. The challenges we face in this millennium are not new and simply germane to a few; we all feel the stress and strain of our economy, whether rich or poor, young or old, male or female. It would be very easy to say, "Why me Lord? Why do I and my loved ones have to suffer?" Most males don't mind a little suffering, but we try everything in our power to protect our loved ones from the effects of trials and challenges.

One of the most distressing things in life for a man is to not have the ability to protect and shield his family and loved ones; to have a sense of hopelessness that he can't do anything to fix this crisis, or correct the injustice with which he is confronted. I think most of us live our lives from the vantage point of wanting to make life smooth for those who fall under our umbrella of responsibility. When I think about the many challenges I have faced in life, I have come to understand that I must embrace the moment of crisis. I don't embrace it with passion or gratitude, but I embrace it to see what I can learn from it and how I can overcome it. Too often we see crisis or challenge as an enemy, and not as a tutor in life. I have come to realize that if I am to overcome the storm I must learn to navigate through the storm and not allow the storm to navigate me to a point of shipwreck.

I have come to the conclusion that life is tough and not always fair. Whether I like it or not, it is a reality. If we don't understand life as it is, we'll keep wishing for something else and most likely never get it. We can complain and pontificate about the way things should be but never will be. The world is not devoted to making us happy; we must decide to accept responsibility for ourselves. This is one of the toughest lessons we will ever learn in life. However, if we choose to accept it, we can live more effectively and proactively.

One of the main differences between those who succeed in life and those who fail is how they approach the storms of life. People, who are prone to fail either try to avoid their problems or work around them. Successful people accept them and work through them. They recognize they are in a storm and understand they have to navigate through the treacherous waters to avoid capsizing and demise. It's a process of meeting our problems head on and looking for solutions that give life purpose and meaning.

The problem that many people face regardless of age, race, or gender is that they really don't accept the fact that life involves a certain amount of difficulty. They fight against it rather than adjusting to it. They complain, moan, and accept defeat as their fate as if they are the only persons to ever suffer trials and tribulations. This type of attitude only makes life and circumstances worse, because it is a way of refusing to accept them as necessary conditions of life.

Men (and ladies), once we accept the fact that life is tough, we begin the process of growth and maturity. We begin to understand that every problem is an opportunity. This is where the rubber meets the road, where we must dig down deep and discover what we are made of and Whose we are. And who are we? We are men who are God-created, ordained, authorized and empowered. Instead of letting the storms of life defeat us, we should welcome them as a test of character. We use them to elevate us rather than deflate us to a point of despair and desperation.

We must be careful because we live in a world that tells us everything is quick, easy and instantly accessible. Television commercials tell us we can win the lottery if we play, become real estate tycoons overnight, lose hundreds of pounds in a flash, and a list of other feats if we just order their product. Many of us are wooed by these types of advertisements because we need and want a quick solution to our dilemma, and advertisers know most people are looking for the quick and easy way out. Winners and overcomers know that life is tough and there are no quick fixes; results come because you have committed the time, effort, sacrifice and pain to endure. Our real success is determined by how well we deal with adversity. What we become in life depends more on our decisions than our conditions. One of the many lessons I have learned in life is that we cannot allow life to control us. We must control our lives, and not allow the circumstances of life to cause us to give up.

Faith is the courage to stand up to the harsh realities of life and say you can't and won't defeat me. I said in the opening of this chapter that we needed faith and action to be overcomers. Once we have the faith then we need to act on that faith. Implement an action plan that says I will not just sit here and let life pass me by. Action says, I now make a decision, no matter what the circumstances are: "I DECIDE TO MAKE THIS UNFAIR LIFE WORK OUT FOR MY GOOD."

When I determine life is not going to frustrate and overwhelm me, then I can move into a posture of being a problem solver. I take responsibility for my life and actions from this point forward. I believe that no matter what the economic indicators say or forecast that God has a plan for your life. Now that you have the resolve to confront life for what it really is, you can begin the process of navigating through the storms that are facing you. I believe you are the captain of your destiny and no storm, trial or challenge is larger than you. There is a greater One who resides inside of you and gives you the ability to overcome every odd no matter how insurmountable it may appear. I dare you to stand up in the face of the 21st century and say, "No matter what, I am going to overcome my economic crisis, my image crisis, my stereotype, my disadvantage." I believe life has given me the opportunity to be an "overcomer" no matter what the odds. Yes, life is tough and can be unfair. You must understand circumstances don't control your destiny; your decisions do. Take time right now and decide to live, to win and to be an overcomer in this life.

YOUR DREAM CAN BECOME REALITY

I would like to say to every person reading this book, dreams can and do become reality. Never let a circumstance, situation or person steal your dream. You were created by God to make a difference in the earth today, and as long as you continue to dream, possibilities and opportunities are at the brink of all you can think or imagine.

Abraham, Moses, Joseph, David, Ruth, Esther, Deborah, Martin Luther King, Bill Gates, Steven Francisco (my beloved brother) and many more were dreamers—men and women who saw what others could not see or were afraid to see. God has placed within you the power to be change agents of destiny; not only your destiny but the destiny of men, women, boys and girls who are depending on you to fulfill your purpose in life. You are more than what "they" said you are. You have abilities beyond your imagination, but it takes faith and trust in God to become the person who God created you to be. I have attempted to open up your mind's eye to cause you to see what's been available to you all the time.

The prodigal's father told the eldest son, "all I have is yours simply for the asking." I believe all that you need is yours simply for the asking and the change to posture your life to become a conduit of God's rich supply. You can be the husband, father, son, entrepreneur, developer, dreamer, mentor or whatever God has called you to be. I encourage you to re-read the chapters of this book and begin to mine nuggets of truth and wisdom as a gold miner would in a gold mine. Chisel and dig deeply into the Word of God and there you will find what you need to sustain your life and the lives of those entrusted to you.

THE CONCLUSION

I call you blessed, successful, and determined and I offer this prayer in conclusion just for you:

> Father, I pray that (_____your name_____)
> will find the keys to unparalleled success in
> the chapters of this book. I pray that You will
> cause them to become the head and not the
> tail, above only and not beneath. I pray that
> divine wisdom will be imparted into them as
> they seek Your word and will, and from this
> moment forth understanding will shine upon
> them as the rays of sun warm the earth, so
> re-ignite the radiance of Your fire in their soul,
> heart and purpose. I believe Your Word that
> says, "nothing will be impossible unto them."
> I pray this prayer in faith, Father, that
> immediate turn around will take place in their
> lives from this day forward and forever more.

Be blessed my friend, take the tools of this book and seize all that God has promised you. This is the only life you get—maximize it—*it's your destiny!*

How to Become a 21ˢᵗ Century Man of God

Throughout this book, I emphasized having a real relationship with God. This is the most important relationship you can develop in your life. It will make all of the difference, not only in your life, but in your family life and in your career and environment. If you are reading this book, and have never truly trusted Jesus Christ as your Lord and Saviour, here is how you can do so today.

1. Accept the fact that you are a sinner, and that you have broken God's law. The Bible says in Ecclesiastes 7:20: *"For there is not a just man upon earth that doeth good, and sinneth not."* Romans 3:23: *"For all have sinned and come short of the glory of God."*

2. Accept the fact that there is a penalty for sin. The Bible states in Romans 6:23: *"For the wages of sin is death..."*

3. Accept the fact that you are on the road to hell. Jesus Christ said in Matthew 10:28: *"And fear not them which kill the body, but are not able to kill the soul: but rather fear him which is able to destroy both soul and body in hell."*

The Bible says in Revelation 21:8: *"But the fearful, and unbelieving, and the abominable, and murderers, and whoremongers and sorcerers, and idolaters, and all liars, shall have their part in the lake which burneth with fire and brimstone: which is the second death."*

4. Accept the fact that you cannot do anything to save yourself! The Bible states in Ephesians 2:8, 9: *"For by grace are ye saved through faith: and that not of yourselves: it is a gift of God. Not of works, lest any man should boast."*

5. Accept the fact that God loves you more than you love yourself, and that He wants to save you from hell. *"For God so loved the world, that He gave His only begotten Son, that whosoever believeth in Him should not perish, but have everlasting life"* (John 3:16).

6. With these facts in mind, please repent of your sins, believe on the Lord Jesus Christ and pray and ask Him to come into your heart and save you this very moment.

The Bible states in the book of Romans 10:9, 13: *"That if thou shalt confess with thy mouth the Lord Jesus, and shalt believe in thine heart that God hath raised Him from the dead, thou shalt be saved." "For whosoever shall call upon the name of the Lord shall be saved."*

7. If you are willing to trust Christ as your Saviour please pray with me the following prayer:

> Heavenly Father, I realize that I am a sinner and that I have sinned against you. For Jesus Christ's sake, please forgive me of all of my sins. I now believe with all of my heart that Jesus Christ died, was buried, and rose again for me. Lord Jesus, please come into my heart, save my soul, change my life, and fill me with your Holy Ghost today and forever. Amen.

For More Information About
Bishop L. W. Francisco III's Ministry, Visit:

www.The21stCenturyMantheBook.com

www.LWFrancisco.com

www.CalvaryCommunity.org

3751490

Made in the USA